How

WAL★MART

is Destroying

America

How
WAL★MART
Is Destroying
America

And What You Can Do About It

Bill Quinn

Ten Speed Press
Berkeley, California

Ten Speed Press
P.O. Box 7123
Berkeley, CA 94707

Distributed in Australia by Simon & Schuster Australia; in
Canada by Publishers Group West; in New Zealand by Tandem
Press; in South Africa by Real Books; in the United Kingdom and
Europe by Airlift Books; and in Malaysia and Singapore by
Berkeley Books.

Text design by Toni Tajima
Cover design by Lisa Patrizio
Illustrations by Ivar Diehl
Printed in the United States of America

Library of Congress Cataloging-in-Publication Data
Quinn, Bill, 1912 May 15-
    How Wal-Mart is destroying America and what you can do
about it /
          Bill Quinn
          p. cm.
          Includes bibliographic references and index.
          ISBN 0-89815-973-3 (pbk.)
          1. Wal-Mart (Firm) 2. Discount houses (Retail trade)—
United States. 3. Retail trade—United States—Personnel
management. 4. Small business—United States. I. Title.
HF429.2.Q56   1998
381'.149'0973—dc21   97-45767
                    CIP

1 2 3 4 5 — 01 00 99 98

DEDICATION

To Lennie Quinn, my wife of over fifty-one years, without whom I couldn't find my way to the bathroom.

To my son Rix, who took over the family publishing business twenty years ago and freed up the old man to write personal stuff, like this anti-Wal-Mart book.

To Phil Wood, president of Ten Speed Press, who shares my feelings on Walton Enterprises...and tells you why in his "letter from the Publisher."

CONTENTS

Why am I publishing this book about Wal-Mart? Well, for a couple reasons. First and foremost is my great respect for author and Wal-Mart hater Bill Quinn. Bill and I go way back, and I consider him something of a publishing mentor. In fact, if he hadn't encouraged me when I was just starting out, I might not be publishing this book of his right now!

Then there's my personal experience with Mr. Walton's empire, which was brief but nasty. To make a long, ugly story short, I had never dealt with Wal-Mart stores, as Ten Speed is a small publisher, and Wal-Mart just seemed too big for us. But, in 1995, a sweet-talking sales rep for Wal-Mart convinced us that it would be good business to sell them books and, indeed, it started out looking that way.

Sam's Clubs bought almost 30,000 books from us, paying us close to a quarter of a million dollars. We cashed the check and started counting our blessings. Then we stopped counting and started cursing. Two months after we'd shipped out all those books, the rep called us up and said the books weren't selling as fast as Sam's wanted, they were sending back everything that was left, and could they have a full refund for the unsold stock please. I was disappointed, but after all, I figured, that's the cost of doing business.

Then the books came back—53 percent of the order! And that's not all-those poor books were sloppily packed into shoddy old food boxes, barely padded, wrapped in something that looked like chicken wire. Not surprisingly, almost 70 percent were so badly damaged as to be unsalable. And Sam's wanted all their money back—$94,583.02 worth! Needless to say, we have not done business with them since, and when the chance came to publish a book that exposed business practices I disapprove of-and have experienced firsthand—I leapt at it. Read this book, marvel at Wal-Mart's audacity, and then fight back! This book tells you how.

Why this bitter anti-Wal-Mart book?

First, Wal-Mart and its subsidiaries have destroyed Small-Town America. Once towns lose their identity, their uniqueness, their mom-and-pop stores, and the young people who look forward to taking over the family business, the towns rarely, very rarely, recover.

Second, Wal-Mart Stores, Inc., (Wal-Mart, Sam's Club warehouses, Hypermarts, and Bud's Outlets) has done more to stomp out Middle-Class America than all other discount houses put together.

Perhaps a little background on this writer will put my pet hate (Wal-Mart) in perspective:

My dad was a small-town railroad agent who prided himself on knowing virtually everyone in the towns where he worked-three in Louisiana and four in Texas. Pa Quinn finally settled in Grand Saline, Texas in 1920. He sank deep roots there, becoming a deacon in the Baptist church and being elected to the school board. At the age of 46, he and my mother built their very first-and only-home.

The second of their two children, also known as me, inherited Pa's small-townitis and, at age 15, I announced to an unlistening world that I was going to grow up to be a newspaper editor. No one believed me, if for no other reason than that I had been the worst student in every grade to date.

Indeed, that ambition had almost faded by 1935, when, at the age of 22, I was finally offered my first journalism job, as editor and publisher of the weekly Van (Texas) Banner. Salary: $60 a month. Van, by the way, had a population of about 800.

By 1940, things were looking better. I became editor and publisher of my hometown paper, the Grand Saline Sun, serving a population of 1,799. Then I got a much better job, editing semi-weeklies in Mineola, a town of about 4,000.

Van, Grand Saline, and Mineola, by the way, form a triangle, 13 miles form each other, down in beautiful East Texas.

Then came World War II, an after serving nineteen months overseas with the Third Infantry Division, I was named editor of a daily mobile newspaper started in Anzio, Italy and, fittingly, called the Beachhead News.

Though I moved my old manual typewriter to Fort Worth some fifty years ago and got into the trade journal publishing business, I continued to run our magazines in a highly personalized, country-newspaper style, making a better-than-average living until I finally retired—at age eighty-four.

The bottom line is, I never left "home"—Grand Saline, Texas. When someone asks me where I live, I still nod my head toward East Texas.

How's Grand Saline doing these days? There isn't a Wal-Mart there. Yet, only thirteen miles both east (Mineola) and south (Canton), Wal-Mart has superstores that have claimed well over half of Grand Saline's retail business.

Grand Saline once had three thriving independent dry goods stores. Now there's none.

The first casualty was a department store owned and operated by my wife's uncle for almost seventy years. The second department store had to close its doors after being in business for over fifty years. The third locked up for the last time on New Year's Day, 1998. Other independent stores in the town have suffered proportionately.

It's been estimated that for each Wal-Mart store in existence, 100 family-owned businesses have gone under. Which adds up to—what?—a quarter of a million mom-and-pop store owners tearfully telling their children there is no money if misfortune comes their way.

What really stirred me up to assemble stories for this book was a 1991 story in *Fortune* magazine. A *Fortune* reporter followed the late Sam Walton around for a week. His impression of the Arkansas genius:

> And finally, there is the ruthless, predatory Sam, who stalks competitors—in any *size, shape, or form* [emphasis added]—and finds sport in blasting them from the sky like so many quail.

Then came Sam Walton's autobiography:

> If some community, for whatever reason, doesn't want us there, we are not interested in going in and creating a fuss. I encourage us to walk away from this kind of trouble because there are just too many other good towns out there who do want us.

What a lie! Clipping after clipping has come to me in recent years from Vermont, New York, Pennsylvania, and Massachusetts, where protesters have organized to try to keep Wal-Mart out.

But fighting Wal-Mart back is worse than David fighting Goliath. One way or the other the Arkansas discounter squeezes its way in—often pressuring courts to decide in its favor—and once in, it can become the town's worst citizen. Always taking, taking, taking. But does it ever give back? Ever?

What Is Wal-Mart?

It's the biggest retailer in the world. (It did over $100 billion in sales last year, worldwide.)

It's the biggest private employer in the United States. As of November 23, 1997, 730,000 people worked for Walton Enterprises. (That's almost three quarters of a million, folks!)

It's a resident of virtually every town or city of any size in the United States and more than 300 towns in Canada, Mexico, Argentina, Brazil, Puerto Rico, China, and Indonesia.

It's a predator. An article in *Forbes* magazine's 1991 "400 Richest" issue laid out the basic Wal-Mart concept as follows: "Discount stores in small towns and rural areas, each big enough to freeze out competition."

7 THINGS THAT HAPPEN WHEN WAL-MART COMES TO TOWN

Let's say it's your town. It's not big, maybe 5,000 to 30,000 folks live there, with all the businesses and services that would serve that many people. Probably, the town's not growing—and that worries some. Some think that a big retailer might help—something flashy to pull in people and money from a wider area.

So now, all of a sudden, there's a 155,000-square-foot "box" store out along the interstate, just barely inside the city limits—but definitely not "downtown." There's a sea of asphalt and a curtain of cyclone fencing where there used to be farmland or a trailer park or woods. Sam's a citizen of your town now, and he's ready to pull in the commerce from thirty-five miles around and more.

Here's what that will likely mean to you and your town.

Store Owners Take the Biggest Hit

If you're a store owner, and your business is directly competitive with Wal-Mart (that is, you sell hardware, pharmaceuticals, general merchandise, whatever), you already know you've got the fight of your life on your hands. Wal-Mart's sheer size gives it incredible advantages.

✪ Wal-Mart's arrival will probably be accompanied by a fair amount of excitement and anticipation. A lot of people in your town will want to have a Wal-Mart. They'll see all the advantages of having a big discounter around, probably without seeing the costs to the town and the life they have known. And you know Wal-Mart is not going to point those costs out to them.

✪ Because Wal-Mart is so darn big, it can cut any deal it wants with vendors and distributors (see chapter 4).

✪ It can lure your customers with claims of convenience and low prices (whether those claims are true is another matter—see chapter 3), offering an easy alternative to the downtown you and your fellow merchants have worked so hard to build.

✪ It can afford to spend quite a bit on advertising and promotion—and you can bet it will. (At first, anyway: read on to find out just how long that spending continues.)

✪ It will engage in "predatory pricing" in an attempt to drive you out of business fast. A new Wal-Mart on the offensive against its local competition will take losses on merchandise that those competitors sell. It'll study what you sell, then offer it for less. Let's say you are Jim, and you own Jim's Hardware in your town. Local Wal-Mart managers will ascertain what you are selling and at what prices; then they will stock, advertise, and sell those items at prices below their cost. You can't possibly compete with this practice without losing money, and chances are good that eventually you will be driven out. Wal-Mart will then be able to sell its hardware merchandise at whatever price it wishes, having eliminated the competition—**you!**

ONE STATE'S DEATH TOLL

A 1995 survey in Iowa shows what Wal-Mart had done to its state since arriving in 1983:

50 percent of clothing stores had closed

30 percent of hardware stores had closed

25 percent of building materials stores had closed

42 percent of variety stores had closed

29 percent of shoe stores had closed

17 percent of jewelry stores had closed

26 percent of department stores had closed

Wal-Mart takes its business overwhelmingly from existing businesses. Townspeople often hope that a big shiny Wal-Mart will pull in commerce from outside the town and bring more money in—and it will—but almost never enough to justify cannibalizing most of a small town's small businesses—which is what happens. On average, over 100 stores eventually go out of business in the area surrounding a "Wal-ed" in town.

Jobs Are Lost

One of the biggest prizes Wal-Mart offers to struggling small towns is the promise of more jobs. If a town is not growing, this sounds really attractive: a great big new store is going to need people to work there, isn't it?

But, for every job created by a Wal-Mart, at least 1.5 jobs are lost, according to the Residents for Responsible

Growth, of Lake Placid, NY. Numerous other studies give similar figures. The biggest reason for this is that Wal-Mart typically employs from 65 to 70 people for every $10 million in sales; other small business employ 106 people for each $10 million in sales. So Wal-Mart can do more business and pay less for employee salaries—and it will. This is one of the great cornerstones of Wal-Mart's success.

Also, a Wal-Mart or other big retailer coming to town is not really offering new jobs in the way a manufacturer would be. People sometimes lose sight of this. If a new factory opens in town, it is literally creating jobs that did not exist before; if a new store comes to town, and that store is selling merchandise that, for the most part, was already available in the town, it is just going to be rearranging the way money already gets spent in the town. What Wal-Mart offers is not job creation, but job reallocation and, eventually, job loss.

It's also worth remembering that many of the jobs Wal-Mart offers are part-time and low-paying. Chances are that a majority of Wal-Mart's employees work less than the customary forty hours a week (the retailer defines a "full-time" worker as someone who puts in twenty-eight hours per week and above). And perhaps 60 to 70 percent of these workers (both full-and parttimers) have no health insurance. All are being paid a low retail wage, and all are subject to work shortage or layoff at the slightest downturn in store sales.

Other Businesses Suffer

Businesses that are not directly competitive with Wal-Mart (the ones that don't sell the same stuff) may have a kind of wary optimism about their big new commercial neighbor. Maybe Wal-Mart will share some of its wealth in town—sort of spread it around.

Don't count on it.

NEWSPAPERS

When Wal-Mart comes to town, it has been known to be a newspaper publisher's best friend. Full-page advertisements! Color inserts! The advertising money that Sam brings feels like a bonanza. But just you wait. As soon as the local drugstores and dry goods and hardware and appliance stores have closed, Wal-Mart may just decide to withdraw almost its entire advertising expenditure from your pages. This pattern was first noted by the Wall Street Journal in a 1993 article.

A national publication once cited two small newspaper publishers who had felt burned by Wal-Mart's abandonment:

✪ In one town in Arkansas, Wal-Mart had gained its desired market share and promptly cut its local advertising down to the bone. Wal-Mart then asked the local newspaper for publicity for its sponsorship of a local event. The publisher of the local paper, who had learned a bitter lesson from his former advertiser, told Wal-Mart to go to hell: "I don't give free publicity to companies that don't help pay the light bill around here."

✪ Another publisher—I believe it was in Snyder, Texas—was invited to come by and get a picture when founder Sam Walton came through the town. "Thanks, but no thanks," he told the Wal-Mart manager. "If we don't have a readership worth advertising to, why should you want us to run a photograph?"

Even in Sam Walton's own hometown of Bentonville, Arkansas, Wal-Mart rarely advertises in the local paper, according to a Wal-Mart director, and Sam's own son owns the paper!

Retail Rapacity Meets the Law—and Loses

Several folks have sent me an Associated Press clipping on the three Conway, Arkansas, druggists who sued Wal-Mart for selling certain merchandise below cost, in an effort to run smaller competitors out of business. Arkansas has a law, the Arkansas Unfair Practices Act, which states that no one can sell any article below cost "for the purpose of injuring competitors and destroying competition." Comparable suits are facing Wal-Mart in other states. Wal-Mart "lost a similar case in 1986 in Oklahoma and was forced to raise its prices," according to the Associated Press.

BANKS

We've been told that it's part of Wal-Mart's overall business strategy to instantly transfer its daily earnings from its stores directly to corporate headquarters in Bentonville, Arkansas. So, while the local bank may have accounts with Wal-Mart, the retailer is just using the bank as a sort of cash drain from the town: pour in the dollars and pipe them out of town the next day. The bank gets no use of the capital this cash might represent, and, worse, the town gets no benefit from it either.

One rule of thumb states that every dollar spent in a small business will get spent again one or more times before it leaves the area (many more if there are not a lot of tourists and other outsiders coming in and out of the area). This means that, if a dollar is spent at Wal-Mart instead of at the local hardware store, not only does the hardware store lose that dollar of revenue, but so might the local hauling company that delivers to the store or the cafe where the store manager has dinner. Instead, that dollar goes directly to the Fort Knox in Bentonville, where it rafts up against billions of other bucks from around the country.

From a larger perspective, Wal-Mart's nonrelationship with local banks can harm a town's growth in general. Small towns often rely upon their banks to be engines of growth: this is where capital meets investors and new business is formed. But if capital is hopping on the morning flight to Arkansas every day, entrepreneurs (that is, potential employers) are left empty-handed, and they'll have to just go away or give up.

TOURISM

Is your town a charmer, like historic Sturbridge, Massachusetts, or Gig Harbor, Washington? Do people come from outside the area to revel in your town's ambiance? You may really want to think two or three times about whether Wal-Mart's big old prefab one-look-fits-all box store is going to be what those free-spending tourists want to see.

In Lake Placid, New York, local citizens did a survey to see what tourists and visitors thought about the proposed Wal-Mart in town. Here are the results:

✪ 94 percent of respondents said they would be disappointed to see a Wal-Mart in Lake Placid (3 percent would be pleased; 3 percent had no opinion).

✪ 95 percent said a Wal-Mart would detract from the appeal of Lake Placid (2 percent said it would add to the appeal; 3 percent said it would not affect the appeal).

✪ 72 percent said a Wal-Mart would make them less likely to visit Lake Placid again (2 percent said it would make them more likely to visit; 26 percent said they had no opinion).

Clear enough?

(By the way, all three of these towns—Sturbridge, Massachusetts, Gig Harbor, Washington, and Lake Placid, New York—have successfully fought off Wal-Mart's approach to their towns—mostly through the organized work of outspoken and tenacious citizens, and sometimes after very hard battles indeed. Your town can do it too: see chapter 7.)

Downtown Dies

This is the all-too-frequent result of Wal-Mart's infiltration of a town—and it's part of the plan. Wal-Mart's formula is to provide a neatly packaged and heavily promoted alternative to downtown.

It is an essential part of Wal-Mart's expansion plan to choose a site that is not in downtown: Wal-Mart builds on undeveloped land away from either a town's established center or business district. Moreover, Wal-Mart's developer normally buys the land at the cheapest possible price, and the land is graded and hard-topped expressly to accommodate them—not to fit in with a town's larger development plan or work in partnership with other businesses in town. Wal-Mart knows where it wants to be and how it operates—not in proximity to other businesses, and not in partnership with other merchants. Wal-Mart is there to destroy the competition and make a buck, not to build community or add to the one that exists.

Wary local activist groups have done studies on what would happen to their local economies if a Wal-Mart came in, and the results are chilling (though not surprising). To quote the Save Historic East Aurora (NY) Association, "Our village [would] strip our retailers, and especially our Main Street business district, of 68 percent of their existing sales" if a Wal-Mart was allowed into the town. Scary!

Taxpayers Pay for the Disaster

These big retail boxes take up a lot of city resources—streets, water, sewer lines, power tie-ins—and a lot of these utilities would be new, because Wal-Mart is, in its ideal plan, building on undeveloped property. You can bet, with Sam's eye on the bottom line, that he is not going to quietly pay for what he uses if he can stick it to somebody else.

Indeed, the *Portland Oregonian* reported that when Wal-Mart opened its store in Lebanon, Oregon, "Things heated up at the city council when Wal-Mart 'suggested' the city make some improvements to its streets, water and sewer tie-ins, and add some traffic lights—a package that was estimated to cost a half-million dollars." This suggestion, remember, was from a discounter who was going to ship the dollars made in Lebanon right out of town the morning after, rarely pausing to invest anything in the town that recently rolled out such a plush red carpet for them.

The New Paltz, New York Planning Board recently did some math on what would happen in their city (fiscally speaking) if they let Wal-Mart build a supercenter in their town. Here are their enlightening findings:

ITEM	
Wal-Mart property tax	+$100,000
Cost of municipal services	-$29,000
Additional services	-$5,000
Tax losses at 3 other malls	-$29,000
50% property tax abatement	-$50,000
Total town tax deficit	<$13,000>

So the town would actually come out losing $13,000 a year, at this conservative estimate. This does not even begin to account for other losses brought about by stores closing, people losing their jobs, and the flight of local cash right back to Bentonville.

You may not be surprised to learn that New Paltz decided not to allow the proposed Wal-Mart in their town. There may be any number of hidden costs attached to Wal-Mart's coming to town, and some of them may be difficult to predict or notice before it's too late. For instance, the town of North Elba, New York, according to the Residents for Responsible Growth in nearby Lake Placid, is allocated a certain amount of hydropower at a fairly inexpensive rate. With the coming of a Wal-Mart into their municipality though, the demand for electric power would probably rise significantly—and so would the price. With one new corporate citizen (that is, Wal-Mart), North Elba would be using far more than its permitted power, and everyone's rates would go up significantly.

Do you think this cost was accounted for anywhere in Wal-Mart's proposal to come to North Elba? I doubt it.

Other Towns Suffer

It's not just towns that actually have a Wal-Mart within their city limits that feel the rippling effects on their commerce and quality of life that the giant retailer brings—and, again, that's all part of the plan. The sales area of a Wal-Mart is about seventy miles in diameter, and one of Wal-Mart's corporate strategies is to "carpet" the land, so that, essentially, the entire country falls within the sales area of at least one Wal-Mart. So it stands to reason that a number of towns will lose commerce to a nearby Wal-Mart without getting much of anything in return. Take my home town of Grand Saline, Texas (population 3,000).

I grew up there. In the '20s and '30s (and '40s and '50s and so on), a person had to look for a parking space downtown: now it's almost empty-and it's even worse on Saturday, which used to be the busiest shopping day of the week. The city sales tax revenue took a 54 percent drop over a twelve-month period. The First National Bank went out of business. Once there were three drug stores, three thriving dry goods stores, three stores selling appliances. Now: one, none, and none, respectively.

Grand Saline doesn't have a Wal-Mart-but Mineola and Canton, both only thirteen miles from my hometown-do. Grand Saline's own businesses have sickened and died; its downtown has shriveled; it's losing its center and becoming a commercial suburb of the Wals in Mineola and Canton. It's hard to watch this happening to the town I love!

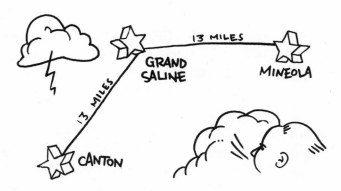

Wal-Mart Moves On

Scariest yet are the tales of woe from the towns that actually were strip-mined by Wal-Mart. A small town's lifeblood just isn't always enough to feed the world's largest discounter—not anymore. Consider the story of Nowata, Oklahoma—brought down not once but twice by Wal-Mart's policies of expansion and consolidation.

Nowata is an oil town of about 4,000 souls in north central Oklahoma. In 1982, Wal-Mart came to town and quickly became the "new downtown." According to an article in the *New York Times,* a collapse in world oil prices and the typically splashy opening of the super-store combined to drive roughly half of the local shops out of business. For over ten years, Wal-Mart was the city's biggest business and, with seventy employees, its second biggest employer.

Then, in 1994, Wal-Mart left, and the city of Nowata was shattered again. This was a town that had sacrificed its business diversity to the "box," and had quickly come to depend on the presence of Wal-Mart in town. The citizens of Nowata, disproportionately poor and elderly, loyally shopped at Wal-Mart, keeping its revenues healthy: an analysis of the store's sales tax payments in the early '90s shows that, on average, the residents of Nowata were spending over $1,200 a year per person at Wal-Mart. Bryan L. Lee, president of the First National Bank of Nowata, where Wal-Mart made night deposits, has said that daily receipts for the store were as strong and steady right before the store closed as they had ever been in the store's history.

So what happened? It seems the good citizens of Nowata—like those in a growing number of Wal-Mart towns across the country—got caught in the next phase of Wal-Mart's growth strategy: "consolidation." In short, the construction of a new Wal-Mart supercenter in Bartlesville, 30 miles from Nowata, meant that two older and smaller Wal-Marts—the one in Nowata and that in Pawhuska, to the south and east—had to go. And the folks who used to shop at those two smaller stores now had to travel to Bartlesville to get their tennis shoes and plastic tackleboxes. (For more about Wal-Mart's supercenter "consolidation" strategy, see chapter 6.)

For Nowata, Wal-Mart's pullout felt like disaster all over again. A lot of people were thrown out of work. Many folks who didn't have cars literally lost the only place they could do some of their necessary shopping. And, due to lost sales tax, there was an $80,000 deficit in the city's 1995 municipal budget of $1.2 million that city officials were left scrambling to bridge. More than anything, the town felt betrayed: Wal-Mart had come in, made itself necessary, then left without notice. Indeed, before the store was closed, Wal-Mart in Nowata posted signs outside: "The rumors are false: Wal-Mart will be here always."

(When asked about these signs, Don E. Shinkle, Wal-Mart's vice president for corporate affairs, said that they were put up "based on market research at the time and the later decision [to abandon the stores] was based on market research later." How's that for firm, reliable corporate policy?)

In some sense, you could say that this is the way things are: Businesses sometimes leave and deliver a crippling blow to the communities they abandon. This is part of the cost of doing business. But in a town like Nowata, cruelly cut down twice by the same massive retailer, that cost just starts to feel too high—and like it all gets paid by the folks with the most to lose.

For the story of Hearne, Texas—another Nowata—see page 82.

Wal-Mart Is a Pill Some Pharmacists Can't Take

Pharmacists are taking up arms against Wal-Mart in Texas and Colorado-and I'll bet other states will soon follow-because of the pressures the Bentonville-based blankety-blanks put on the guys and gals we trust with our lives when they fill our doctors' prescriptions.

In Houston, fifteen pharmacists sued for overtime pay. In addition, four pharmacists say that Wal-Mart supervisors "subjected them to changing schedules and frequent embarrassment in the workplace and in front of coworkers," said a recent Associated Press story in our local papers.

In 1995, three Colorado pharmacists "accused the company of devising a policy requiring pharmacists to work 45 hours per week without overtime pay." And, the next year, a sister lawsuit was filed in Colorado accusing the discounter of having a "sweatshop mentality."

One of the Houston pharmacists, Jennifer Miles, is now "on medical leave, receiving treatment for anxiety and depression that she says was caused by the 'intimidation campaign,' " so says the Associated Press article.

1 SURE-FIRE WAY WAL-MART BARGES INTO TOWN
(AND 3 WAYS IT SNEAKS IN)

Sam Walton claimed that one of his bedrock business principles was never to build in a town where Wal-Mart was not wanted. This was probably an easier thing to do way back in the day when Sam and Company were just beginning their pattern of world domination. Back then, towns didn't know what they were inviting in, and what Wal-Mart was selling sounded pretty good.

Things are a little different in the 1990s: now there are scores of private anti-Wal-Mart groups throughout America; the majority of these are citizen activist groups in specific small towns where Wal-Mart has planned a store. Some of these groups have taken their messages on the Internet; and many of them have received a fair amount of visibility in the national press. The word is finally getting out about Wal-Mart's effect on a community, and the retailer is finding more and more towns that say, "We don't want you, Wal-Mart!"

A couple of good anti-Wal-Mart Web sites to check out are run by Al Norman's Greenfield, Mass.-based "Sprawl-Busters," at www.sprawl-busters.com; and the Peninsula Neighborhood Association of Gig Harbor, Wash., who created an "Us Against the Wal," www.harbornet.com/pna/page1.html walmart, site to publicize their (successful!) fight to keep out the big retailer.

But, in the words of New York developer John Nigro, who has worked to bring Wal-Mart into some of their targeted towns, "[the big retailers] know what they want." If Wal-Mart wants to come into your town, and it knows just where it wants a store to sit, Wal-Mart will come to town even when faced with a helluva fight—even when faced with towns that do not want Wal-Mart and say so.

Location, Location, Location

To paraphrase the old real-estate saw about what makes a property desirable, there are really only three things Wal-Mart needs to move into a town:
(1) Zoning
(2) Zoning
and (3) Zoning

The master plan for Wal-Mart, wherever it goes, involves the "box": the classic Wal-Mart square, prefab, ugly monstrosity of a building surrounded by asphalt parking lots as far as the eye can see. Uniform architecture and site-planning is one of the keys to the retailer's scary success—no surprises; every place is the same. It's like mass production.

In coming to a town, Wal-Mart will fix its eye on a certain parcel or parcels of land that will fit the bill: undeveloped and outside the downtown or other business district, with plenty of room for parking and easy access by the highway or other major roads.

Often, Wal-Mart will find its dream parcel, but it's not zoned for the kind of heavy-duty retail use Wal-Mart wants it for. So Wal-Mart has to get that zoning changed before or at the same time that it applies for a business permit. And often this is not such a big task. Wal-Mart and its developers are pros at this, and have prepared documents that show the city council and the planning commission that Wal-Mart will be the best new citizen of the town imaginable, and that this parcel of land was made to be Wal-Mart's new home. (These proposals tend to be studded with what one Wal-Mart critic has dubbed "Wal-Math"; that is, "they only know how to add": more jobs, more community involvement, local buying, positive response to local needs—the whole phoney-baloney ball of wax.)

Understandably enough, this is the best stage for people who don't want a Wal-Mart in their town to stop it. The Lancaster County (Pennsylvania) Planning Commission put together a succinct summary of the steps small towns should take in "Wal-Mart-proofing" themselves. (Thanks, folks. This is dry stuff, but useful as hell.)

✪ Adopt urban growth boundaries; in other words, limit the area in which urban-level development can happen within the town, and make those boundaries clear.

✪ Review local comprehensive plans; a town's comprehensive plan is a document that sets out the goals and policies for a town's desired growth pattern. This is a town's statement of what it is and what it wants to become, and it can be a powerful document in fighting against outside developers who have their own ideas about what should become of the town.

✪ Review zoning ordinances; a town's zoning ordinance should be consistent with the town's comprehensive plan.

✪ Review subdivision and land development regulations. These regulations specify what a developer has to demonstrate about the nature and impact of its proposed development. Make sure the regulations are strong and detailed enough to give your town a clear picture of any proposed development—from the developer itself.

Here's Your Hat—What's Your Hurry?

In one county, the discounter wanted to take over a mobile home park occupied by 170 residents so it could build a136,000-square-foot supercenter. The company's original offer to the residents if they'd relocate? Two hundred big old American dollars. "This isn't fair," said one resident who had lived on the site for four and a half years. No, my friend, it's not.

As you might guess from the above, it's not so easy anymore for Wal-Mart to just waltz into a town with its usual bag of tricks. The words "Wal-Mart is coming" are like a red flag for lots of citizens who have seen what havoc the monster retailer has wreaked in other towns—and who don't want any such thing happening to their town.

So Wal-Mart has had to evolve some ways to get around this new defensiveness. God forbid they should just say, "Oh, okay, small town, you don't want us, so we'll go elsewhere." I've pinpointed three of Wal-Mart's oleaginous new ways—all sneaky as can be, and all listed below.

Dateline North Carolina

T. R. Taylor and his wife wanted a house away from downtown that they could settle in for life. They found the perfect spot back in 1940—a one-and-a-half-acre wooded plot. They built their house and cleared some trees for a garden. Decades went by before their dreams were shattered. The Taylors now have a Wal-Mart built around them, ruining the property they have been on since 1940. Wal-Mart bought the land next to theirs and bulldozed around their house, leaving them 20 feet up a bank, with a ditch 30 feet across and 300 feet long separating their property from the superstore. An insulting offer was made for the Taylors' property—an offer that they turned down. Even the line of trees that was supposed to buffer the house from the development never materialized. The Taylors' son sums it up thusly: "Human beings do not do this to other human beings."

Manipulate Existing Zoning

In Virginia, Wal-Mart was able to come up with an absolutely ingenious way to get around not one but two sets of municipal codes at once. Here's what happened: In the town of Warrenton, city code said that any retail outlet over 50,000 square feet had to have special permission to be built. When the Wal came to Warrenton, it naturally had to ask for such permission to put in its proposed monster: a 120,000-square-foot box. Properly alarmed at the thought, the city said no, that's just too big for us. And it would seem that Wal-Mart was beat: they asked and got turned down.

Now, Fauquier County, which surrounds the town of Warrenton, has a similar code on its books, stating that retail outlets exceeding 75,000 square feet in size have to be approved.

But voila! Wal-Mart found an appropriately zoned parcel that straddled the line between Warrenton and unincorporated Fauquier County, and the discounter

---

Does Wal-Mart Hold Nothing Sacred?

A friend in Hawaii faxed us a front-page story in the *Honolulu Advertiser* about Wal-Mart trying to build "on land that should have gone to long-suffering Hawaiians who have been on the waiting list for homestead lands for decades." You can bet that Wal-Mart will get out their slime buckets and throw every possible drop at anyone and everyone who crosses them in building one of their box stores on land that rightfully belongs to Hawaiian natives.

---

was able to get around both sets of restrictions by putting less than 50,000 square feet of its box inside Warrenton land, and less than 75,000 square feet on Fauquier County land, for a grand total—still—of over 120,000 feet! Local courts found that the use was permitted—or at least was not excluded—by the available laws.

Thirteen neighbors of the proposed Wal-Mart development appealed the ruling that this arrangement was legal. One of them, Deborah Gortenhuis, said in an interview with the *Washington Post*, "I think it's sort of sneaky that they want to do this thing. Wal-Mart tries to depict themselves as this very honest, family-oriented, small-town kind of store. But with all this sneaking around, you wonder about that. They seem ruthless."

Use a Front Man

This is a damned effective technique. From what I can see, it's one of Wal-Mart's favorites. Check it out.

Some aware citizens in Evergreen, Colorado, suspected that Wal-Mart was scoping out their town for a possible location. So on several occasions they called Wal-Mart headquarters and asked them what their development plans were for Evergreen. Each time the reply was the same: "We are not looking at real estate in Evergreen."

Meanwhile, a real estate development company from Denver has appeared before the county zoning board, asking for rezoning on a couple of parcels. They don't own the parcels, but are interested in getting them rezoned, then acquiring them for later sale or lease to Wal-Mart. In this way, the path will be paved for Wal-Mart to come in, and local citizens who would wish to keep it out have lost one of their most powerful weapons in the fight: strict zoning restrictions.

A similar sort of thing recently happened in Arroyo Grande, California, where Wal-Mart, when asked, had repeatedly said it had no plans to come. At the same time, a developer was pushing through the necessary zoning changes for an unnamed store, denying to town officials all along that their client was Wal-Mart. The developers were busted when a citizen came forward with a copy of a sell/lease agreement signed months before by Wal-Mart and the developer.

Yet again, I hear that the city council of Ithaca, New York, unanimously voted to spend $3,600 in outside lawyer fees to keep Wal-Mart from building a store just inside the city limits. Seems a development company from South Carolina, working on Wal-Mart's behalf, had secured a conditional zoning variance from the city to build "an unidentified store." When the city found out the store was to be a Wal-Mart, they said no. Now they are fighting to keep the Wal out of their town.

Let this be a warning to would-be Wal-Mart busters: keep an eye on rezoning requests that would make a parcel Wal-Mart-ready, no matter who brings the request. You don't know who's really behind it.

Papa Sam Disrespects the Father of Our Country
Does Wal-Mart respect any rule of decency? When they announced their plan to build a supercenter on George Washington's old Ferry Farm where, 'tis said, he chopped down that cherry tree, a resident's group begged the retail giant to build elsewhere and, instead, donate the site for historic preservation. "This is very naive," said Jay Allen, Wal-Mart's vice president for corporate affairs. "We're going ahead."

Hell, Use a Straw Man

This is the only time I've heard of Wal-Mart using particular tactic, and I can see why. It sure is not the kind of situation a big old strong international conglomerate retailer wants to find itself in more than once—embarrassing!

In Greenfield, Massachusetts, Wal-Mart was facing quite a battle from a grassroots citizen's group that wanted no part of the retailer in their town. In what can only have been a state of desperation, the retailer set up a phony citizen's group called "The Citizens for

Economic Growth," which started running pro-Wal-Mart ads in the newspaper. When the anti-Wal-Marters called to find out who was on this new citizens' committee, they got no reply. A little further sleuthing revealed that "The Citizens" were (1) Wal-Mart's lawyer, (2) her secretary, and (3) her secretary's boyfriend.

Well, maybe Wal-Mart only abandoned this type of ploy because they got caught at it so darned easy. Pathetic!

"Give Not"—So Say the Waltons

Fortune's February 2, 1998 issue contained the magazine's listing of the "40 Most Generous Americans." The biggest contribution, of course, was Ted Turner's, billion-dollar gift to the United Nations, and to environmental and family planning groups, through a private foundation. The smallest contribution in the "40 Most..." list was $12 million, given by William Warren for a classroom building for Columbia University.

Was the Walton family, some $35 billion rich, mentioned among the 40 multimillionaires who want to give something back to the people who made them the wealthiest families in the U.S.? No. Not only no, but hell no. Can you imagine, even remotely imagine, a family that wealthy who has yet to contribute one-tenth of one percent of its annual income to an American charitable institution?

3

2 WAYS WAL-MART IS OH SO GREEDY

I'd like to start this chapter out with parts of an interview I conducted with a former Wal-Mart manager; a man who had been on the inside of the beast for over fifteen years. A lot of what Joe [not his real name] has to say speaks to the top 2 Ways Wal-Mart Is Oh So Greedy.

BQ: Joe, your wife tells me your hours as a manager were so long you barely knew your children?

Joe: Long hours were demanded—rarely less than seventy a week, most weeks eighty or more. Days off were rare. And I have gone as long as three years without a vacation. My wife literally raised our children by herself.

BQ: Hourly workers, I've been told, are held to a minimum?

Joe: You won't believe how they are treated. Managers try to keep employees' hours under twenty-eight a week so they won't be eligible for benefits.

If business slows on any day, managers are instructed

to send workers home any time after they have four hours on the clock. Even department heads who are supposed to be regulars can be sent home, ofttimes working less than the thirty-seven and a half hours they are entitled to.

BQ: Is it better now than it was?

Joe: No, worse, I've been told. When a regular employee quits now, managers are instructed to hire two part-time people to take his or her place.

BQ: This is a personal question, and you may not want to answer it. But how much did you make as a store manager?

Joe: You'll laugh at this. But before I quit in the 1980s, I made $15,000 a year, but I could draw up to $15,000 against my annual bonus, which I normally had to do. Most I ever made was $35,000. And I was considered one of their better managers, constantly on the upgrade, getting better stores.

BQ: When you moved, did Wal-Mart pay your expenses?

Joe: No. Actually, the "system" was to ask store personnel to do you a favor by working off the clock to come out to your place and help you pack. You were moved to your next assignment, always, in a Wal-Mart truck. And at your new station you asked for volunteers to come out and help you unpack. Never on company time. Always off the clock.

BQ: What about real estate you might leave behind?

Joe: Wal-Mart headquarters always bluntly told you they were not in the real-estate business. Had never been. Would never be. And, on our next-to-last move, we took a helluva loss on our home.

BQ: Suppose you told your regional manager you were happy where you were and didn't want to move?

Joe: That wouldn't work either. It was always a larger store, paying a little more. But in spite of that, I told my boss one time I wanted to stay where I was. Then I got a call from the vice president of stores from my area to suggest, in the strongest terms, that I start packing. It was as simple as that. If I refused, I was out the door, fired, through with my future at Wal-Mart.

Why didn't I quit? I've asked myself that a thousand times. But one gets to doing something, knows he's good at it, and feels, ultimately, that things will get a lot better. I don't know why I didn't get the hell out sooner, but when you've got a family and lots of years invested, you just stay with the company.

BQ: In traveling from place to place, the company paid car expenses, didn't they?

Joe: That's another area where Wal-Mart is chintzy.

Chintzy beyond belief. My mileage refund on one of the years I remember was 11¢ [a mile]. My wife was working at the time, and her company car allowance was 22¢ a mile. Double my allowance!

BQ: I've heard that when you had annual meetings to which your wife was invited, they wouldn't allow you to use your own car?

Joe: That's another not-so-funny joke. I remember a couple of those widely-touted "family" affairs the company called "Wal-Mart Ballyhoos." Always by bus.

Four or five managers would drive their own cars to a central Wal-Mart store, load up, travel on to the next central pick-up point, pick up another group, and so on until the bus was loaded to the gills. We went up to one meeting in Missouri that was a fourteen-hour bus drive. Got up at 5:00 A.M. to catch the bus. No stop for lunch. And, everyone was required to bring their own sack snacks. Once there…tired, tired, tired…no refreshment bar.

Then two days of intense meetings, 7:00 A.M. until almost midnight. Then, on the fourth day, back on that damn bus for home. And on that fifth day, you had better be back to work— on time.

On another of these trips they said it would be at the rather nice Hot Springs Majestic Hotel. Not for us. It was a Day's Inn, a long, long walk to the Majestic, where our meetings were held.

BQ: When you opened a new store, what happened?

Joe: We were instructed to go into a town to dominate! Dominate! Dominate! First job was to shop the competition. I had a full-time person for that. I particularly remember [town name deleted].

My lady shopper would come back with their prices, dictated into a hidden microphone. We'd cut their prices a penny or two. If we got into real warfare with a Kmart or Target, we'd send our people over to their stores to buy as many of their sales items as we could…and brought them back and sold that product for a little less. We even shopped the mom-and-pop hardware and drug stores. Our job was to destroy the competition, large and small, in every way we could. If a mom-and-pop store couldn't stay in business—their problem. Never, never was there a more ruthless bunch of blankety-blanks than Wal-Mart.

BQ: Were you encouraged to belong to local civic organizations?

Joe: Yes. We were encouraged to join and be as much a part of that organization as possible, but always at our own expense. I was never reimbursed for any of the money I spent that way. But, for sure, Wal-Mart emphasized that their key personnel were a part and parcel of their respective communities.

BQ: What about charitable contributions in the towns you were in?

Joe: Wal-Mart had a simple strategy for that. When someone came in for a contribution, you welcomed them with open arms and told them store policy was simple: Just write a letter on their organization's letterhead, and you'd be glad to send it to company headquarters that very day. A week or two would go by, and, if asked, you'd tell the solicitor that, "Well, you know how long it takes a request to go through the channels in a company as big as Wal-Mart." Then, a couple of months later, all would be forgotten. The job of the manager was to be nice, nice, nice to those people who come in for a contribution to their cause.

BQ: I've heard awful stories about how mean Wal-Mart can be to its vendors.

Joe: That's one of the reasons I had to quit them. I had one lady whose job was to make claims of product damage, or claim that the full order was not received, pallet damage, whatever. The company's policy was to make a vendor prove the full order was sent. On damage, they had to believe our claim—or lose Wal-Mart as a customer. You can't believe the number of claims an average Wal-Mart store makes in a single year. Not one store. All stores.

BQ: What about local vendors?

Joe: When we bought from a local vendor, except for utilities, of course, we were instructed to deduct 10 percent. Don't ask me for what. If we had to call in someone to service something, same thing. Quite often the invoice would be held if there was the slightest question. Normally, the local vendor would allow us to take the 10 percent. I was against all this—to the fullest. But those were our instructions.

Let me add here that all of those petty claims against virtually all vendors were not written instructions, always verbal. So far as I recall, I've never seen anything written on Wal-Mart stationery on which they might face suit.

BQ: What part of your job was most unpleasant?

Joe: Being responsible for hiring personnel. And working them just as cheap as you can get by on. My guess is that the Wal-Mart employee of today is even worse off than he was some twenty years ago, when I went to work for them.

I'd say that 80 percent of their workforce is in the minimum wage area. I think you'd be surprised how many of them are on food stamps or some other assistance.

BQ: Newspaper friends have told me that when a new store goes in, they're good advertisers, but once the store is in, advertising levels off.

Joe: I know that for a fact. They go all-out to beat down the competition, demand certain positions in the local paper, use fractional pages with no other advertising on the page. They know every trick of the trade. Demanding, demanding of everybody.

But once they dominate the competition, it's usually a once-a-month circular or insert. No newspaper could exist if all the stores in town were like Wal-Mart.

BQ: What was your worst experience at Wal-Mart?

Joe: Being sent into a town with instructions to fire the key people—often for petty infractions of company policies. Things like that tug at your heart.

BQ: When you finally quit Wal-Mart, were you fully vested?

Joe: I thought so. I calculated I had $30,000 coming. But you can't believe the add-ons they had on my final check. Administrative expenses, deductions I never dreamed of. The final amount was only $5,000. I should have sued, but that would have entailed legal expense, and like all claims against Wal-mart, it would have been in the courts forever.

BQ: What was your actual reason for quitting?

Joe: My conscience was eating me up. My normal weight is around 200 pounds, and I was down to about

145. My deepest concern was that I was selling every moral I ever believed in.

BQ: Would you say Wal-Mart is dishonest?

Joe: I don't know how to answer that. I do know they take advantage of virtually everybody who has ever worked for them. I do know that they take every advantage of their vendors. I do know that they take advantage of every customer who walks into their store.

My greatest regret in life is that I ever tied up with Wal-Mart in the first place. And I know in my heart that if you interviewed every former manager of Wal-Mart, the vast majority of them would tell you an almost identical story [to the one] I'm telling you today.

Clean-Up On Aisle Nine: Will the Nearest Shopper Please Assist?

This from a September 1997 feature story in the *Wall Street Journal:* Wal-Mart in "Irving, Texas has posted signs on its doors asking customers to bring in a shopping cart from the parking lot. For their troubles, shoppers can enter a weekly drawing for a $10 gift certificate." Note it's a weekly drawing, not a daily one. One $10 prize! Wow! How can a family worth almost $35 billion afford to share their riches so generously?

So, without further ado, here are the two biggest ways I've found that Wal-Mart Is Oh So Greedy:

Employees Are Wrung Dry

You've heard the war stories of one former Wal-Mart manager, Joe, who gave so many years of his life to a company he now regrets ever hearing of. Sadly, Joe's story is not unique: Many Wal-Mart employees ("associates," as they are called) are honorable, capable, hard-working folks. It's too bad their big boss pretty much sees them as bumps on his bottom line.

It is widely acknowledged that one of the great keys to Wal-Mart's formidable success is its lower-than-low cost of doing business. Wages in particular are low as can be. Compare Sears to Wal-Mart in this area. According to *Value Line*, Sears pays its employees 24 percent of its sales. Wal-Mart is down to 16 percent. Every gear in the whole vast machine is straining to keep costs down, profits up, and growth exploding. Of the hundreds of places Wal-Mart can (and does!) save money, its workers' hides are the favorite.

Minimum wages and minimum benefits: that's the way Wal-Mart stays ultra-competitive. Here are a few more "features" of working for the world's largest retailer:

LOW PAY, SCANTY HOURS

Retail jobs pay the least of all categories of employment tracked by the U.S. Census Bureau: lower than service, lower than mining, certainly lower than manufacturing.

These wages are approximately 39 percent lower than the average wage, and a full-time retail wage normally puts the earner well below the federal poverty line.

So the people who work at Wal-Mart are not looking at the rosiest picture to start with. Then, remember that many Wal-Marters work part-time (the company doesn't release employment data, so we don't know how many). Now realize that Wal-Mart defines "full-time" as twenty-eight hours per week or more, and you'll see a workforce where the actual majority does not work a regular, forty-hour work week at all. Many—too many—Wal-Mart employees must be on food stamps or other government assistance.

This reality can be a bitter pill for folks in some towns who welcomed Wal-Mart, with its promise of additional jobs. Wal-Mart will hire you, all right, but you may not be able to afford to shop in the store very often.

It's a Bird!...

Wal-Mart's consuming desire to save warehouse space by stacking merchandise to the ceiling in its stores has begun to cost the discounter. I have here in my hand a clipping about a $435,000 suit Wal-Mart lost when a thirty-pound box fell on a former nurse. Her attorney presented telling evidence to the jury, saying, "25,000 cases have been filed against Wal-Mart nationwide involving customer injuries resulting from falling merchandise."

THE DISPOSABLE WORKER (I)

Even "full-time" Wal-Mart workers have no job security: count on that, none, zippo, zero. Regular employees are subject to having their hours cut any time, any hour of the day, when business slows down, as an article in *Inc.* magazine's July 1994 issue reported. Managers are under pressure to keep staff levels in line with the flow of business, and often this is done on the fly, midshift. Makes it a little hard to plan the old household budget, doesn't it?

And if business overall slows down: Well, forget about it. In the words of one of their suppliers' reps, Wal-Mart operates on the basis of sink or swim; and they don't care if you sink. Just keep hoping that Bentonville HQ doesn't shut down your whole store.

...It's a Plane!...

In Corona, California, one lady was seriously injured when a shelving unit at Wal-Mart fell and pinned her to the floor. Two others were slightly hurt in this accident and were treated at a local hospital. The husband of the seriously injured lady criticized Wal-Mart's handling of the situation: "The manager of the store didn't talk to me. I had to find out myself. They're going to have to pay the medical expenses—but all I have is a phone number." If this painfully injured lady tries to get a little money for her suffering—including medical expenses—I'll bet the Wal-Mart organization will try to fight her case all the way to the Supreme Court.

...It's a Motorized Ice-Fishing Augur, Falling on My Head!

"Watch Out for Falling Prices," says Wal-Mart in their TV ads. Really, you'd better watch out for falling boxes from their ten-foot-high stacks of merchandise—so stacked because the company is too cheap to have adequate storage space at their stores. But after thousands of cases of falling merchandise that resulted in injuries in the past five years, Wal-Mart may soon have to start making their stores safer for shoppers—particularly in Denver. That's where Phil Scharrel was injured when a forty-pound box containing a motorized ice-fishing augur fell ten feet, hitting Phil on the head and causing permanent injury.

Phil sued, as he should have, and the jury awarded Phil and his wife $3.3 million. Wal-Mart is appealing the award, of course.

THE DISPOSABLE WORKER (II)

In Plattsburgh, New York, Wal-Mart opened a brand-new store around the Christmas holidays in 1993. By the end of January 1994, the company laid off thirty of their new employees a mere month after the opening. These people did not know they were just being offered seasonal jobs. Happy Holidays from Wal-Mart!

> ### Just So You Know
>
> Here's what might happen should you get injured in a Wal-Mart store. Widow Phyllis Benoit went into a brand-new Wal-Mart in Westfield, Massachusetts. Mrs. Benoit slipped on a wrapped Hall's cough drop lying in the aisle, did a split (ouch!), and fractured her hip. The manager helped her get a wheelchair, and she was taken to the hospital—where hip replacement was promptly ordered. Eleven months later, Mrs. Benoit was still in pain and had medical bills of over $35,000: Wal-Mart told her attorney in no uncertain terms that the store was not responsible for her accident and would not help with medical expenses. Sad news, indeed, for a widow living on her $629 monthly Social Security check.

ROTTEN HEALTH BENEFITS

An October 1996 *Wall Street Journal* article showed just how bad Wal-Mart rates in the matter of health care for its employees: it's the lowest of the low.

According to the *Journal*, the company's euphemistically named "Personal Choice" health plan has such strict rules for eligibility—and such a high cost to the employee—that only 43 percent of employees were covered in 1995. The retailer requires that an employee must work at least twenty-eight hours per week (remember, twenty-eight hours per week is Wal-Mart's definition of "full time") and have been employed at Wal-Mart for at least two years. So that means the 30 percent or more of Wal-Mart employees who are part-timers aren't eligible at all.

Then, on average, Wal-Mart employees pay about 35 percent of the cost of their health plan—much, much more than the national average, which is 20 percent, according to the United Food and Commercial Workers Union.

This Is WAL-TV

Sometimes I think Wal-Mart must have a senior vice president in charge of screwing its suppliers. October 1997 financial pages tell of the Bentonville blankety-blanks introducing vendor-sponsored in-store cable channel commercial that would play only on sets on display at its (give or take) 2800 locations in the United States.

Suppliers Are Squeezed

Wal-Mart has a lot of clout: a nice fat order from the mega-retailer would seem to be the dream of many manufacturing concerns. Wrong, wrong, wrong!

Because Wal-Mart is so big, it can (and does!)

demand just about anything it wants from its vendors, from deeper-than-usual discounts to downright disadvantageous shipping policies to enforced returns on slow-moving merchandise. Some manufacturers are getting to the point where they just say "no" to doing business with Wal-Mart: the huge sale to them is not worth the even huger headache.

So here are some of the things Wal-Mart does to its vendors so often these practices begin to feel like unwritten policies.

CLAIM SHIPMENT DAMAGE WHENEVER YOU CAN

Remember my interview with Joe, the former Wal-Mart manager who finally quit after over fifteen years? He told me how he had one employee whose job it was to claim product damage, or tell vendors that the product was not received, or that the pallets it came on were damaged.

In fact, this was one of the policies that made him finally feel he had to leave Wal-Mart: the way vendors were forced to prove they sent their full order of merchandise. And when Wal-Mart claimed damage (which was often), vendors had to take Wal-Mart's word on it— or lose a huge customer.

Quite by accident, I overheard a conversation that seemed to imply that there may be something a bit fishy about Wal-Mart's damage policies. Two food brokers from different companies had sold to the mega-retailer: both were evaluating whether they were actually losing money by doing so. The reason? Wal-Mart's tendency to deduct alleged damage on shipments. They are "worse than all the others put together," said one of the brokers.

Dog in a Manger

This is a story about a small business in Texas that thought it could coexist with Sam. It was wrong.

Hot Diggity Dog, a hot dog vendor owned by a woman named Scarlett Rabelais, was doing all right. Between 1987 and 1991, Scarlett had contracted with Sam's Wholesale Clubs to sell hot dogs outside eleven Sam's stores in Texas. Scarlett gave Sam's 10 percent of the gross sales for the privilege of setting up outside their doors, and she bought the food for Hot Diggity Dog from the wholesaler.

According to radio commentator Alex Burton, the problem came when Hot Diggity Dog started making some money. Sam noticed and said he'd like to buy out the company. Scarlett said no, and Wal-Mart ordered the vendor off its land.

Here's the kicker. Scarlett's ninety-two employees were all elderly or handicapped people who would probably be on welfare if not for their Hot Diggity jobs. That Sam Walton would be willing to throw these people out of business because he couldn't get all the profit from their work shows just where his idea of community and social responsibility is: not one step over his own bottom line.

What was that you were saying about the cost of welfare being too high, Mr. Walton? Would you care to do anything real about it? Didn't think so.

U.S. WORKERS SOLD DOWN THE RIVER

How much does Wal-Mart care about buying American? These two paragraphs from Al Norman's Sprawl-Busters Alert, July 1997, answer that pretty well:

> In Newburgh, New York, the Wal-Mart store was picketed by members of the Professional Workers Association after 290 workers were laid off by the Hudson Valley Tree Company. It seems Wal-Mart canceled its contract with the American manufacturer of artificial Christmas trees. Hudson Valley Trees says that it lost its contract because Wal-Mart, which boasts of its 'Buy American' program, opted instead to purchase artificial trees from China.

> According to the AFL-CIO, late last year a Native American (Indian) company went out of business on the St. Regis Reservation in northern New York after Wal-Mart decided not to carry its fishing lures. Officials at the Mohawk-owned Kanenkeha Lure Company urged a boycott of Wal-Mart. Kanenkeha employed eighty people at its peak.

Made . . . Where?

Remember those "Made in America-Keep America Working and Strong" signs that were so prevalent in Wal-Mart stores and advertising in 1991? "A smoke-screen to bring in more imports," claimed a former manager (and probably all of his competitors). Smoke-screen must have been right. China's imports more than doubled between 1991 and 1995, according to the import figures we saw in a national magazine.

PENALIZE VENDORS WHEN MERCHANDISE DOESN'T SELL

The National Apparel Bureau has got wind from its members that Wal-Mart has been forcing an extra discount from them on merchandise that doesn't sell. The Bureau's president says he has received:

> numerous complaints from vendors [saying] that the discount retailer was demanding a 'markdown allowance' of between 4 and 10 percent [for merchandise] Wal-Mart purchased from them but couldn't move...and (using) the threat of reprisals, including ending their business relationship, if vendors didn't comply.

You may want to circle the above paragraph and send it to folks in your industry who are selling to Wal-Mart or Sam's Club. If they haven't got caught in this slimy practice yet, they're probably just lucky.

Some of Wal-Mart's Tricks for Wringing Out a Few More Bucks (according to Business Week)

- ✪ Calling a supplier collect

- ✪ Asking for huge numbers of free samples

- ✪ Asking for discounts for new store openings

- ✪ Commissioning cheap knock-offs of successful brand products

...and so much more!

From the Pulpit

Sam Walton and Wal-Mart, ever my nominees for the scum of mass-merchandisers, are even getting pulpit criticism down in my part of the country.

A preacher here in Fort Worth, Dr. Barry Bailey, senior minister of the 10,000-member First Methodist Church for some sixteen years, had a several-minute segment on the greed of Sam Walton and Company in a Sunday sermon heard in several states via cable in 1992. Several quotes from Barry's broadcast:

- ✪ What is passing for competition in America today is greed.

- ✪ There is a strong company in America today that owns many stores, many outlets.

- ✪ One of the wealthiest men in the world owns this company.

- ✪ He started small. You can read about it and be exuberant about the fact that someone can be broke and still make it in America.

- ✪ You can sell this, but I do not like the way the company is being run.

- ✪ I have not liked it for a long, long time, in part because of the way I have seen little county-seat towns dry up.

- ✪ We are free to shop where we want to shop; that is right.

- ✪ But there is a lot more to it than just making money when one store, with its bigness, makes it and little stores cannot make it.

- In this mammoth organization that I happen not to be thrilled about, what he often does is not work his people long enough for the organization to pay their insurance, their hospitalization.

- They work a limited number of hours.

- They get little (or no) benefits.

- He is cutting out the middle man so he can sell to you cheaper.

- Is that really what you want, cheaper?

- Is buying cheaper the only thing that matters?

- Then you have just one big store in America and everyone else is unemployed.

- Is that what it is all about?

- I thought service was pretty good.

- I thought decency, a fair wage and helping your employees were pretty good.

- Greed; there is a lot of difference between greed and competition.

- Cheaper, by itself, is not enough, is it?

- Ask a bigger word than that.

- This is America, and you have to take care of yourself.

- You are not even taking care of yourself when you destroy the people who were your customers.

- There are other words that ought to come in rather than just, "What did you pay for it?"

CANCEL ORDERS IMMEDIATELY WHEN BUSINESS SLOWS

When sales reports tell the headquarters in Bentonville that sales are weak, vendors tell me Wal-Mart is notorious for canceling orders or refusing shipment on orders right away. This disregard for manufacturers is the sort of thing that can send smaller or less-prepared suppliers into serious trouble—even bankruptcy—on Wal-Mart's whim.

RENEGE ON VENDOR CONTRACTS

The *Wall Street Journal* reports that in the mid-1990's, the athletic-shoe maker L.A. Gear took a nasty sales hit when Wal-Mart cheaped out on a vendor contract with the manufacturer. Wal-Mart had made an agreement to buy at least $80 million of merchandise from L.A. Gear. Instead, according to the *Journal,* Wal-Mart would buy only about $45 million worth. Anybody placing bets that Wal-Mart then gave the supplier a break on their agreed discount for that merchandise? Not me!

FORCE DISCOUNTS ON SUPPLIERS

As you may know, many suppliers offer a 2 percent discount if bills are paid within ten days of invoicing. According to *Forbes* magazine, Wal-Mart usually pays its bills closer to thirty days—but routinely takes a 2 percent discount even then. What's more, Wal-Mart takes the discount on the gross amount of the invoice rather than the net amount, which deducts for costs like shipping—larger amount, larger discount, and bad, bad manners from a company with the clout to throw its weight around like this.

USE A LITTLE SUBTLE INTIMIDATION

An executive of our acquaintance recently made his first visit to the buying offices of Sam's Club. There, among the unfinished plywood walls and folding tables and chairs, were signs greeting you, hollering "How Low Can You Go?" Well, at least you know where you stand going into the interrogation, er, negotiation.

Pennies from Heaven

Newsweek ran a story in October 1995 about a certain loophole the Wal-Mart family seems to have found in the federal tax code. Take a look at this one. It's a beauty.

A provision in the tax code called Corporate-Owned Life Insurance (COLI) was designed to help small businesses—mom and pop shops, and the like. The big-shots at Wal-Mart insure over 250,000 of the company's employees under COLI; and Wal-Mart, not the employee's kin, is the beneficiary-even if the insured is no longer a Wal-Mart employee. And the Wal is not liable for any federal taxes on the benefits.

The scheme is financed by the same insurance company that sells Wal-Mart the policies. The retailer borrows the cash to pay the premiums on COLI and borrows separately (also from the insurer) to pay the interest payments on those loans. Talk about cozy! It's a closed circle: Wal-Mart benefits, and so does the insurer; Uncle Sam and the insured worker's next of kin get nothing.

---

4

6 REASONS TO BEWARE OF WAL-MART

It's no secret I hate Wal-Mart. They've been under my skin for more than fifteen years now, and I do not love them any more than I ever have—which is not at all. Want to know another of the many things I hate about Wal-Mart? You can't trust them any more than you could trust Satan with a snow cone. Here's why.

Promises, Promises

Once upon a time, when Wal-Mart had fewer than 200 stores, Sam Walton called a managers' meeting. The wife of one manager, fearing that the chain would one day open seven days a week, was assured by Sam himself that two things were certain (no, not those two things):

✪ The chain would never, ever, ever open on a Sunday.

✪ The chain would never, ever, triple never sell alcohol, in any form.

(Remember, Sam's other never, ever rule, that he'd never, ever go into a town where Wal-Mart is not wanted? If you wonder what became of that rule, you might want to go back and look at chapter 2.)

What can Sam have been meaning, to make promises like this, that he was never going to keep? Look what happened:

Retailers in the small town of Pella, Iowa, have long observed a day of rest on Sunday. Wal-Mart had been in town for nine years and seemed to respect this taboo. Then suddenly, orders came from headquarters in Bentonville: The store must open between twelve and five on Sunday. So much for the corporation's promise—and so much for sensitivity to local feelings.

But it gets worse.

Wal-Mart, by its own policy, is now universally open on Sundays, unless prohibited by a state or local law. This pretty much forces the competition to open on Sunday, too, if they want to stick around. What is more, Wal-Mart employees with strong religious beliefs have been forced into an impossible dilemma: work on their Sabbath or lose their job.

According to the *Wall Street Journal*, Scott Hamby worked at Wal-Mart in Bolivar, Missouri—until he was fired for refusing to work on Sunday, preferring to go to church. According to Hamby, his manager's reaction to his situation was to tell the woman in charge of setting staff schedules to "keep Scott here on Sunday until he quits." Hamby, a devout Christian and a graduate of

Southwest Bible College, needed his job but cherished his convictions still more. He felt he had no recourse but to sue. A court in Springfield, Missouri, sided with Hamby.

In the wake of this lawsuit, Wal-Mart is being forced to change its policies to accommodate those who prefer to worship someone other than Sam on Sundays. The *Wall Street Journal* also notes that this settlement "could have far-reaching implications for other companies with weekend staffing needs that conflict with workers' religious practices."

Guess Sam met his match this time.

But what about liquor?

Oh, yes. Well, since Sam made never, ever promise number two ("Wal-Mart will never, ever sell alcohol, in any form"), Wal-Mart has become, by some estimates, the biggest nationwide purveyor of beer and wine.

So, two solemn pledges, two utterly broken promises. I do wish those other "dependables" (death and taxes, that is) were this easy to get around, don't you?

Let's Keep an Eye on This One

Newspapers and TV stations down in my neck of the woods have been reporting Wal-Mart's selling used merchandise as new. Steve Gardner, a former Texas assistant attorney general, is asking the courts to certify his lawsuit as a class action, claiming that Wal-Mart and Toys R Us "were regularly and intentionally selling returned goods that were used, damaged, defective, or missing parts."

Always the Low Road

A few years ago, you may have noticed that Wal-Mart mysteriously changed its slogan. The discounter had been promising us "Always the Low Price. Always" for years. Suddenly it became "Always Low Prices"—which still sounds pretty good, I guess, but why the switch? Did something change in the way Wal-Mart does its pricing?

Well, no. Wal-Mart just got caught out, that's all.

The National Advertising Review Board, which is funded by the Better Business Bureau, investigated the claim that Wal-Mart always has the low(est) price. The Board found that this just was not and is not true, and promptly ordered our pals in Bentonville to stop saying it.

Walton Family Values

The *San Francisco Review,* March/April 1997, tells about the second-grade schoolteacher who asked her class whether they thought a woman could be president—and only two students answered yes. Which prompted this teacher to design a T-shirt adorned with the slogan "Someday a Woman Will Be President."

Somehow or other, some of these shirts got into a Wal-Mart store—but were immediately yanked from the shelves because of complaints that such a sentiment goes "against family values."

Untruth in Advertising

Michigan's attorney general brought suit against Wal-Mart for alleged violations in the state's consumer protection act. According to the *Wall Street Journal,* Michigan's attorney general discovered that Wal-Mart's in-store advertisements were misleading: They "compared products that were not the same size or model without noting the difference, and…the ads sometimes inflated the prices competitors charged." Wal-Mart settled, agreeing to various changes in the way it compares its prices to those of competitors. Hey, how about honestly and accurately, for starters?

It also may interest you to know that it is "against store policy" to jot down prices in a Wal-Mart. That's what Virginia Berger of Spring Hill, Florida, was told when she was accosted in a Wal-Mart doing just that, according to an AP wire story. Mrs. Berger, who lives with her husband on pension and disability benefits, says she was "angry and embarrassed, and I thought they were going to throw me out." She later found no problem in writing down prices at Kmart or Target. What is the meaning of this, I wonder?

The Liars' Club

Another major cheek-burner for Wal-Mart's execs (as if they actually get embarrassed): In Missouri, the attorney general blew the whistle on Walton Enterprises' misuse of the word "wholesale" in its Sam's Wholesale Club division. Folks pay $25 for an entry card to this discount nirvana. But is it a real wholesale operation? Not by the hair on my chinny-chin-chin, ruled the AG. And behold, what is this division of Wal-Mart now called? That's right: Sam's Club.

WHOLESALE, EH? NOT ACCORDING TO THE ATTORNEY GENERAL!

Made in the USA? No Way

This is, I think, one of the most astounding stories I've come across in almost fifteen years of Wal-Mart jousting. This made my hair stand on end and stay that way—just because Wal-Mart is so brazen.

It starts, like so many things do, with one of Wal-Mart's creepy corporate slogans. "We buy American whenever we can" is the official line of top dogs in Bentonville, Arkansas, USA. And like so many of their utterings, this line makes it look like Wal-Mart is doing a good thing ("We buy American!") while offering them a way to do whatever suits them, really ("whenever we can"). Because who is to say when Wal-Mart "can" or "can't" do any old thing? Wal-Mart, of course. It's genius.

So far, this is just corporate doublespeak. You and I recognize this; it doesn't surprise us; we wouldn't trust it as far as we could throw it. Now comes the sleaze.

In 1992, Wal-Mart was engaged in a heavy-duty, red-white-and-blue marketing campaign called "Buy American." Patriotic, sentimental TV commercials carried the message of an armada of Wal-Mart stores stuffed to the rafters with goods made in the USA. American flags, red, white, and blue bunting, and signs trumpeting "Made in the USA" wooed shoppers in every store with the same patriotic message: Wal-Mart buys U.S.-made goods; buy at Wal-Mart.

David Glass, Wal-Mart CEO, in an interview with NBC's Brian Ross, claimed proudly that "[we] can make merchandise in this country as efficiently and as productively and for every bit the value that they can anywhere else in the world." Sounds great, doesn't it? Yet, according to *Forbes* magazine, Wal-Mart's Chinese imports coming through *just one port* (Long Beach) totaled 22,000 containers in 1992. This is the same year "Buy American" was at a fever pitch! Talk about a sleazy sales pitch! Wal-Mart's imports *from China alone* then more than doubled by 1995—to 47,000 containers. A conservative estimate for 1997 puts the figure at 52,000 containers—and that's just through Long Beach, which handles only 26% of Wal-Mart's Chinese imports.

CHINA ... CHINA ... BANGLADESH ... KOREA
WHERE'S THE STUFF THAT'S MADE IN
AMERICA?

To get a good picture of this, remember that a railroad flatcar holds two containers. When I was a kid and my Dad, a small-town railroad agent, let me take railroad car numbers for his daily reports, I learned that a flat car measured about 100 feet long. So...a train long enough to haul all of Wal-Mart's 1997 Chinese imports would be 1,893 miles long! A train long enough to reach from Portland, Maine to Miami, Florida. And, of course, this is only the Chinese imports—and the Walton empire imports from dozens of other nations too.

When Brian Ross and his *Dateline NBC* team (with their hidden camera) entered a Wal-Mart store plastered with "Buy American" signs, they found, well, a lot of foreign-made clothes. Articles made in China, Korea, Bangladesh, and Hong Kong were racked under the deceptive "Made in the USA" signs, but nothing actually made in the USA was to be found. These results held true in eleven stores the team visited in Florida and Georgia.

So *Dateline* visited David Glass in his office and presented him with a child's jacket manufactured in Bangladesh that they found racked under a "Made in the USA" sign in Wal-Mart. Mr. Glass's opinion? "That would be a mistake at the store level....You'd be foolish to put a garment that said 'Made in Bangladesh' on a rack that was signed 'Made in America' and believe that you could fool people." Well, odd, because that seems to be just what Wal-Mart was intending with its outrageously phony "Buy American" campaign.

In a separate incident during this time, a union local in New York state put up two $500 cash prizes (one for the union's membership, one for the general public). The goal: see who could come up with the longest list of countries from product labels in the nearby Wal-Mart. The winner came up with forty countries in sixty short minutes.

Apart from fooling the consumer (that's you and me, friend), Wal-Mart had a few other skeletons in its "Buy American" closet. You might want to peruse chapter 5 for more dirt in connection with Wal-Mart and its foreign manufacturing.

Santa or Scrooge?

While Wal-Mart is believed to be dead-last, percentage-wise, among major discounters in charitable giving, it is always ready to make speeches about "giving back to the community" and wring some publicity out of whatever tiny gestures it makes. Here's a couple of for-instances.

When Hurricane Hugo hit Homestead, Florida, in the mid-1990's, Wal-Mart was very noisy in pointing out its $1 million donation in goods. What Wal-Mart was not so eager to publicize was that the donation was a joint venture with some of its vendors, with the goods shipped on Wal-Mart trucks for high visibility. When Wal-Mart was asked to name the vendors who participated, the retailer refused.

I've often wondered if Wal-Mart Stores, Inc., or the Walton family give even 1 percent of their annual income to charity. After Ted Turner pledged to give

$1 billion to UN charitable causes, *Newsweek* gave a partial rundown on what the rich have given to charity and other worthy causes in recent years, and I took a minute to look for Wal-Mart or the Waltons on the list.

First, I scanned through the list of the top foundation givers. Nope. The worlds' largest company was not named. Come to think of it, I've never read anything of the Walton family even having a foundation. Do they?

Second, I checked out the top corporate givers. No mention of Wal-Mart here.

But I remembered reading somewhere else that of the fifty largest businesses in the United States, Wal-Mart was dead-last in sharing the wealth, so that makes sense.

Third, I skimmed the list of 1996's top philanthropists. Not a single one of the $35-billion-rich Waltons here.

What do these people do all day long? I found myself wondering, take baths in asses' milk and plot the takeover of the world?

Dirty Tricks-R-Us

The courts are getting wise to the unprincipled antics of Wal-Mart. According to the *Wall Street Journal,* two suppliers were awarded $7.1 million in a civil fraud. The *Journal* reported that Wal-Mart "committed fraud by requesting under false premises that the women turn over their business records and by turning those records over to a competitor that it has already decided to hire in the first place." Yucch! Looks like it's best to be on the lookout for the worst kinds of tricks from my least favorite discounter.

Yes, Wal-Mart takes every opportunity at their stores to tell folks they are good citizens. I ask, where is the gol-danged proof?

Royko Weighs In

You think I get nasty with Wal-Mart? The late Mike Royko, the nationally syndicated columnist, really dealt that crummy discounter a haymaker in his column. Seems Eric Mattys of St. Charles, IL, bought some tires for his pickup from a Sam's Club store. He was told to come back in forty-five minutes. When he came back, the man who had put the tires on was gone—and so was the truck. The man was traced and found the next day with the truck—which was stripped. He had sold the mirrors, toolbox, stereo—everything that could be sold. The pickup wouldn't run, and Eric had to pay $220 to get the shell of the thing towed home. So back to the store he went. A manager gave him a claim number. It turns out that Wal-Mart stores are self-insured. So Eric called Bentonville. The man he talked to tried to intimidate Eric, saying the truck had been stolen by an individual and he "couldn't believe I [Eric] was trying to make a claim against Wal-Mart." Mike ended his column with nothing but contempt for the multibillionaire members of the Walton family. "So while going to the bathroom at 3 A.M., the interest income of a single Walton would earn enough to buy Eric a good used truck. People can be so greedy. God bless Wal-Mart," Mike concluded.

5

7 WAYS WAL-MART IS BAD TO THE BONE

I'm really started up now, and some will say I ought not to have got started. I think Wal-Mart totes a sorry bag of tricks, and I've got their number: here are seven more ways, big and little, why Wal-Mart is bad through and through.

Sweatshop Labor

Back in the last chapter, I promised we'd come back around to the ways Wal-Mart's "Buy American" campaign meant more than fooling the consumer.

Beyond the hyped-up patriotism and the downright hypocrisy of the red-white-and-blue "Made in the USA" banners in Wal-Mart's "Buy American" promotion were foreign-made goods. Made in Hong Kong, China, Korea, Bangladesh, Central America—these goods are manufactured overseas to get the cheapest possible cost of production, then shipped to the United States to be sold in our markets.

Because labor can be bought so incredibly cheap overseas, especially in Asia and Latin America, this is often the way retailers in the United States can offer fantastic bargain prices on apparel and other goods and still make some money. And some would say there's nothing wrong with that: that's business. And consumers demand a good bargain, so what's a retailer to do? Especially one that only wants to pay twenty-five cents of labor costs on a $19.95 pair of pants. As American union official Jeff Fiedler said in an interview with NBC, maybe Wal-Mart's slogan should be "We buy American whenever we can, except when we can get it in Bangladesh, made cheaper by kids."

And remember Kathie Lee Gifford's tears of embarrassment when she found out that clothes sold under her label at Wal-Mart were sewed by teenage and younger girls in sweatshops in New York and Central America? That news coverage was just a rare shaft of light into a common practice—whatever Wal-Mart's bigwigs may say. (How could Kathie Lee not have known her dress line would be made in cheap-labor countries?)

Charles Kernaghan's report before Congress's National Labor Committee in 1995 gave the following description of conditions at the Global Fashion plant in Honduras, where thirteen- to fifteen-year-old girls were sewing those $19.95 Kathie Lee (Gifford) pants for Wal-Mart for thirty-one cents an hour, seventy-five-hour workweeks, without health care; girls were permitted to go to the bathroom only twice a day; workers were not permitted to talk to each other.

Investigative reporters at NBC had no problem finding twelve-year-old Bangladeshi children sewing shirts for Wal-Mart for as little as five cents an hour; Wal-Mart's CEO called their claim unsubstantiated.

The truth is, said a customs insider, if you buy manufactured goods from Bangladesh or from a number of other countries, you can put your hands over your eyes, ears, and mouth all you like. You still know at least some of those items were made by children working under appalling conditions.

Aside from the usual "that wasn't us, we didn't do that"-type stuff Wal-Mart had to say on the topic of sweatshops, I've managed to glean one other official comment on this deplorable issue. Lee Scott, Wal-Mart's executive vice president for merchandising, spake thus:

"The sweatshops issue is a very big, complex issue, and addressing it in a substantial way is bigger than one company or one person. I'm confident we can make some improvement, working with the rest of the industry." Spoken like a man, Lee.

The bottom line is this: Whether Wal-Mart's hundreds of overseas agents—and their big bosses back in Bentonville—claim to know it or not, little kids are making it possible for the Waltons to be one of the richest families on earth. And by me, that stinks.

"Gray Market" Merchandising

It's happened more than once: A "gray-market" product, made or imported in a way that breaks U.S. law, is
available at Wal-Mart, demonstrating that, at the very
least, Wal-Mart is very sloppy at checking on its suppliers' claims and warranties about their goods.

In 1993, the attorney general of the state of Florida
cited Wal-Mart for selling inferior Seiko-labeled watches
and falsely telling customers that the watches carried
Seiko warranties. Really, the watches had been manufactured and imported without the manufacturer's
consent. When the *Wall Street Journal* called Wal-Mart
about the story, a spokeswoman wouldn't comment on
the allegations.

In fact, it was something like the above sort of practice that first led me to criticize Wal-Mart in print. That

was back in 1983, when I noted in the *Wall Street Journal* that Nike, the athletic shoe and apparel maker, charged Wal-Mart with trademark infringement, unfair competition, and trademark dilution. In short, Nike got ripped off. The federal suit alleged Wal-Mart was selling clothing with fake Nike trademarks. Nike sued, and won.

Nearly fourteen years later, it's mind-boggling to see that Wal-Mart got caught doing the same thing. In 1996, a federal judge in Richmond, Virginia, found Wal-Mart and its Chinese supplier guilty of design patent infringement against...Nike! The codefendants, Wal-Mart and supplier Hawe Yue, had to cough up $6 million for copying and marketing Nike's Air Mada outdoor shoe. The court also issued an injunction prohibiting either codefendant from selling any more copycat Nike shoes. But I look back to the suit in 1983 and I have to wonder: do the greedy ever learn? (I do know who feels responsible: Wal-Mart officially stated that all blame and liability rests with its vendor, Hawe Yue.)

Incidentally, Wal-Mart is believed to have a standard paragraph in nearly all its foreign vendor contracts that the supplier is liable for any judgments or settlements brought jointly against them and Wal-Mart. Just another way Wal-Mart tries to avoid responsibility (and expense) at the cost of anyone, including its business partners.

Quota Busting

Dateline NBC, in their terrific 1992 exposé of Wal-Mart's foreign merchandising practices, uncovered one more way the retailer squeezes a few more slimy cents out of a sale: quota busting. This is a practice in which suppliers, especially in China, manufacture way more inexpensive garments than they are legally allowed to export, then sew tags in them that indicate the clothes were made elsewhere, and unload them on the U.S. market—with the help of retailers, including Wal-Mart, ready to turn a blind eye. U.S. customs authorities in Hong Kong say that even after Wal-Mart's top agent in Hong Kong was warned one of his suppliers was engaged in quota-busting, it made no difference. Wal-Mart just went on buying these questionable goods.

How Loyal Is Your Local Wal-Mart to Your Home Town?

Likely enough, not very, according to Vanessa Asken of the Revolutionary Movement bike shop in Americus, Georgia. Her town's Wal-Mart had a tent sale promotion in which cars were sold (with Wal-Mart of course getting a percentage of the sale). Did the Bentonville, Arkansas monster have any of the four Americus car dealers participate in the tent sale? Nope! Instead, a nearby Columbus, Georgia, dealer was invited to display—and sell—on-site.

Overcharging the Consumer

This is an insidious practice, and more mass merchandisers than just Wal-Mart are guilty of it: they have an outrageous number of price-scanner mistakes. An NBC undercover team found that, up to 10 percent of the time, there are overcharge errors on tickets at discounters, including Wal-Mart. And three out of four times, the error is in favor of the store! This may be due more to sloppiness than malice, but you can bet if the ratio worked the other way (if the customer benefited 75 percent of the time), Wal-Mart and the other discounters would find a way to clean up their act.

Promote American Products!
(Unless the Japanese Pay You to Do Otherwise)

During 1997, Wal-Mart turned its back on Kodak—as American a company as can be. Japan's Fuji Film Company paid Wal-Mart $200 million to take over the photo finishing operations at Wal-Mart stores, with Fuji getting extra profits from its use of its own paper and chemicals—plus preferred shelf space for Fuji film in all Wal-Mart and Sam's Club stores.

"It's stunning news in the industry," said one photo consultant. Most people in the industry expected Kodak to win this contract. It was a second loss in a short period for Kodak on the Japanese front: The American film company had also recently lost a bid for U.S. sanctions against Japan for what it claimed was Fuji's success in locking it out of a big chunk of the Japanese market.

Gats for Tots

Wal-Mart has been forced in recent years to give up its practice of selling guns to anyone who wanted one, in the wake of a few embarrassing incidents. In Fort Worth in 1992, George Lott randomly shot and killed two lawyers in a Tarrant County courtroom with a gun he bought from Wal-Mart. The Wal-Mart salesclerk just had him fill out a form, but Lott neglected to mention that he was under felony indictment. Then, in a South Texas town, a man walked up to a Wal-Mart gun counter and filled out a federal reporting form; in this case he did disclose the fact that he'd received treatment for mental problems. Didn't matter; the clerk sold him a pistol anyway—and the man went home and killed his parents.

Wal-Mart made a lot of fuss about not selling handguns anymore (it does still sell handguns by mail order, and displays rifles and shotguns); but it's been getting into trouble over a related issue. Seems Wal-Mart's in-store regulation of ammunition sales is as sloppy as its handgun efforts were. Another suit arose in Iowa out of an incident in which a teenager walked into Wal-Mart, bought ammo without being asked the necessary legal questions, walked back home, and shot himself.

Candid Camera

Here's a tale from Al Norman's *Sprawl-Busters Alert* August 1997 issue:

A man bought a $400 camera from Wal-Mart. "I took a couple of rolls of film back there, and while looking at them I showed the lady at the counter...a scratch across all the pictures, and she said it was 'a bad lens' and I should return the camera. I said, 'Great, I got it here a few weeks ago.' She said they couldn't take it back, and to return it to the Kmart down the street without the receipt, and that Kmart would give me the money...and for me to come back and buy a new [camera]." Is this not business ethics—and customer service—at its lowest level!

Snakes Alive!

A good old boy in Pleasanton, Texas got a rattlesnake bite instead when he reached for an automotive air filter in a Wal-Mart store. I'll be damned if the Wal-Martians didn't claim he planted the snake there, but the fellow's attorney found that that particular Wal-Mart store had previously experienced snake problems from a nearby open field. Rather then settle this truly legitimate claim out of court, Snake Headquarters fought it in court; I'm pleased to say our hero finally received a $6,000 settlement.

Wal-Mart: "A Bad Neighbor"?

When you are a huge rich company and all you really want is to get huger and richer, it turns out that a lot of smaller, poorer people may have to get hurt in the process. Wal-Mart, with all its size and power, could hurt people or help them in a lot of situations. Which do you think it usually chooses to do?

County surveyor Jay Poe knows. "Wal-Mart is not a very good neighbor," he told the press when a drainage problem behind Huntington (Indiana) High School, created by land now on Wal-Mart property, was ignored by the discounter. The problem was caused when a Wal-Mart developer commissioned the store's landscaping. The landscaper terraced the planted green area incorrectly, and when it rained, the water seeped into the neighboring school's walls and severely damaged the tiles. "Fixing the (school's) tile is not our concern," concluded the developer. Schoolchildren's well-being is not important to Wal-Mart?

Recent events in Washington state found yet another Wal-Mart spokesman saying these same old words again: "I can assure the community that Wal-Mart wants to be a good neighbor." Uh-oh, what did it do now that it needs to make excuses for?

Wal-Mart secured thirty-eight acres to build a store in Central Kitsap, Washington. The site was right next to a tributary of Steel Creek, and heavy rains were due, according to local residents. Nevertheless, despite warnings, Wal-Mart, its developer, and its contractor decided to go right ahead moving earth to hurry construction.

Sure enough, the rains came, and the construction

site's newly graded dirt and silt piled into the creek, wreaking untold damage on the ecosystem of salmon, eel, and grass beds. According to environmental officials, it may be years before the habitat can recover from this senseless, easily preventable devastation.

While the state's Department of Ecology levied the largest fine in the state's history against Wal-Mart ($64,000), locals think that's not good enough. "We need to ask why the company took this risk. Perhaps it didn't matter to Wal-Mart," opined an editorial in the *Central Kitsap Reporter*. I think that writer has something there, don't you?

A Rotten Record with Women and Minorities

Just a few items here, but I think they speak to the way things are at my favorite store to hate.

According to the *Wall Street Journal*, Wal-Mart shareholders recently decided they would not begin to report publicly on the progress of the company in employing women and minorities. Many other large companies post this kind of report. What are the Wal-Mart shareholders ashamed of?

Julie Deffenbach knows. She was a jewelry department manager at a Wal-Mart in Fort Worth. She was a good employee and was singled out for praise when her department did over a million dollars in sales. Julie is also white—a fact which only becomes interesting when you learn that three of her managers, over a lunch meeting, told her she "would never move up in the company by seeing a black man," her fiancé, Truce Williams. But Julie married Truce, and about a week later, she was fired.

When Julie brought suit against Wal-Mart, the jury awarded her $119,000 in damages. Wal-Mart still denies the charge that Julie was fired over her interracial relationship and is appealing the jury's decision. (How I do love to see Wal-Mart stew!)

Wal-Mart claims it doesn't discriminate against black women. But an all-female jury in Houston thought otherwise when they awarded Angela Natt $1.4 million in damages in an August 1997 decision.

On the basis of outstanding performance reviews and regular raises, Mrs. Natt, a Wal-Mart employee since 1988, sought to move into management, on the basis of having men managers with much less seniority than she had.

"When she was finally promoted to manager of the automotive department of the Texas City, Texas, store in 1993, supervisors and other employees berated her with derogatory terms," according to the *Wall Street Journal*.

"She also received harassing phone calls and threats, such as a black monkey being hung over her work area," said her attorney, Eddie Krenek.

Mrs. Natt said the stress became so unbearable that she miscarried her second child, and her marriage ended. She was fired two days after returning from sick leave after the miscarriage. And now the pitiful part: it took four years for Mrs. Natt to get her story before the jury.

Wal-Mart, as it's done in every case that it's lost (at least that I've heard of) is appealing. My best guess is that Wal-Mart will finally settle out of court for pennies, and

I do mean pennies, on the dollar. When? Again, my best guess is that Wal-Mart's attorneys will sit on the settlement until well into the next century.

"Chainsaw Al" Has a Friend in Alice Walton

Probably the most feared man in all of industry is Al "Chainsaw" Dunlap.

He's the guy, you'll remember, that went into such companies as Lily-Tulip, Crown-Zellerbach, and Scott and immediately fired thousands of people. He's now at Sunbeam. And in the first three companies mentioned, he's gone away rich, rich, rich.

"Chainsaw Al," when he went into Sunbeam in 1996, did the usual: Fortune's January 1997 issue says that he eliminated sixteen of twenty-six factories, five of six headquarters, and fired half of the 12,000 employees.

His greatest admirer, probably, is Alice Walton, daughter of Sam Walton, and also president of the Llama Company, one of two investment banking firms "Chainsaw Al" has called in for his expansion program...which will probably be a merger with another big company that Al can chop (chomp?) on.

Explains Alice: "The vendor base to the mass merchandisers is consolidating. The big-box guys have gotten together, and if you're too small, you don't have the ability to serve the largest retailers." Wouldn't you hate to work for somebody who thinks like Alice?—or "Chainsaw Al"?

6

2 WAYS WAL-MART IS A MENACE TO AMERICA AND 2 WAYS THEY WILL TAKE OVER THE WORLD

In a grand sense, every fact and story in this book is about some way the mega-retailer puts the screws to an America that many of us still hold damn near sacred. When the commerce of a small town is casually destroyed, when cheap sweatshop goods from overseas are sold under the banner "Made in the USA," when 1.5 jobs are lost for every new one that comes into town with a Wal-Mart, you could say these are all ways the Wal-Mart corporation has hurt America.

But here, for good measure, are just a couple more stories about how the Walton family has been known to shaft Uncle Sam (that's you, the taxpayer), using the federal treasury to help stuff the coffers of the fabulously wealthy Walton family.

Tax Hijinks

USA Today reported that Wal-Mart owes the feds nearly $32 million in taxes on losses the chain reported over four years. The problem is that, in order to write off losses due to theft, damage, or clerical errors, Wal-Mart actually has to prove the loss to the IRS; the feds want a physical count.

Nope, says Wal-Mart, we can't do it. We're too big. It's just not practical. Geez, why can't you just trust us on this? The last time I checked, the IRS was not buying that one.

Nice to see, isn't it, that sometimes even the biggest bully on the block meets a real...mean...dog.

Oh, Canada...

Dateline 1992: Wal-Mart, new in Canada after buying Woolworth's subsidiary there, "has already stepped on some cultural sensibilities," according to the *Wall Street Journal*. A Montreal newspaper reported that Wal-Mart was requiring 750 managerial personnel...to log an extra twelve hours a week without a salary increase."

Wal-Mart "is the model of savage capitalism," growled the president of a Quebec foundation.

Pork-Barrel Treats

How's this for a great big glistening piece of pork? Early in 1997, NBC's *Dateline* reported the plan to build a $70 million cargo airport in Highfill, Arkansas—just fifteen miles from the Bentonville headquarters of you-know-who.

And you-know-who is footing the bulk of the bill for this international cargo port in the middle of nowhere, too. That's right: you and me. Those are federal funds paying for the quick and easy import of goods made by neither you nor me. I sure hope those legislators on the appropriations committees are enjoying their campaign contributions.

Incidentally, did you ever know that about 15 per-cent of Bill and Hillary Clinton's net worth comes from Wal-Mart stock, and that Hillary Clinton served for eight years on Wal-Mart's board of directors? Yes, the mega-retailer has friends in high places: call them the First "Sam"ily, if you like.

Enough with the petty innuendo, though. I've got a copy of Wal-Mart's 1997 Annual Report in my hand, and it is a smoker. (You ever read one of these things? Scaaaarrry stuff! Makes me wonder if the folks who are writing this actually believe themselves, or if they just close their eyes and think of England, or whatever, the whole time.)

Right here in this shiny document I have outlined for me the scoop on what's in store for the world's biggest retailer. In short, a future I can name with con-fidence (drumroll please):

Supercenter Invasion

Remember, from back in chapter 1, the town of Nowata, Oklahoma? This was the little town whose perfectly adequate Wal-Mart was being pulled out from under its feet because a new supercenter was opening in (sort-of) nearby Bartlesville. Supercenters are Wal-Mart's new Big Thing, and the retailer is "relocating" a lot of their old Wal-Mart stores—closing them down and coaxing customers to come to the new, better, bigger, shinier supercenter not (too) far away.

These supercenters typically include not only the whole range of goods that a regular Wal-Mart might contain, but also such things as a supermarket, an auto service depot, a bank branch, a shoe repair shop, a video rental shop, a pharmacy, a restaurant (such as McDonald's), and more. That is, just about every segment of a typical town's small business commerce that Wal-Mart did not try to move in on before, the supercenters go after.

Oh to Be a Fly on the Wal...

According to the *Wall Street Journal*, "Wal-Mart's (annual) meetings stand out in part because its extravagance clashes with the penny-pinching culture of a company that sets the thermostat of each of its 2,500 stores at the head office....The proceedings are often less informative than hokey. At the meeting following Mr. Walton's death in 1992, an employee took the stage and pretended to converse with him in heaven. The employee said Mr. Sam wanted everybody to sing 'God Bless America.' They did."

Why is it necessary for Wal-Mart to consolidate its current stores into a smaller number of bigger stores? Really, it's a necessary outcome of the pattern of growth Wal-Mart has set in the last ten to fifteen years. Wal-Mart has reached market saturation in many of the regions where it started, mainly the south and the Midwest. What that means is that Wal-Mart stores have "carpeted" the landscape of rural America at regular intervals and have consolidated up to one-third of the retail trade in such states as Mississippi. (That is, one out of every three dollars spent in retail in Mississippi is spent in a Wal-Mart.) Sales growth at these stores is slowing, because much of the competition is gone, and Wal-Mart in these areas enjoys as much of a slice of the market's dollar as possible, given the goods and services that a typical Wal-Mart supplies.

CASE STUDY OF "RELOCATING": HEARNE, TEXAS

If you think I've been saying some harsh things about Wal-Mart, you should listen to what the people of Hearne, Texas, think of Sam Walton's family company.

A Wal-Mart store moved into the outskirts of Hearne in, or about, 1980. Since then, one by one, virtually all the stores on Main Street have closed, and Wal-Mart has become the main game in town. Now, one would think that with half of the town's business coming its way, Hearne's Wal-Mart would become a permanent, prosperous fixture.

Hardly. With the Texas economy slipping, Hearne's Wal-Mart dropped from 115 employees down to 90.

Then came a bombshell. In 1990, the Bentonville, Arkansas–based discounter announced it would be closing the store, claiming the company had been losing money all the ten years it had been in the area, which just has to be 100 percent baloney. What happened, of course, was that Wal-Mart has opened some much larger stores, in nearby cities, that would enable Wal-Mart to close its lesser dollar-volume outlets.

So, says Wal-Mart in essence, to hell with Hearne.

Listen up to some Hearne residents on their feelings:

✪ Archer Hoyt, a drugstore owner is bitter, bitter. "When he (Walton) came in the whole pretense was 'I'm for Little Town America and I'm going to give you some of the benefits that big cities have.' Now he's gotten the cream of the crop out of the county, and then he ups and leaves."

✪ Dave Cunningham, president of the Hearne Chamber of Commerce, doubts Wal-Mart's claim that the local store lost money for the ten years it was in Hearne. Cunningham feels Wal-Mart's closing puts something of a stigma on the community. He says, had the store closed after the first year, "We'd still have a vital downtown."

✪ Burt Lockhart, who runs a store his father opened thirty years ago: "They breeze into town and suck up all the business, then with all the businesses gone, they pick up and leave."

✪ Salesclerk Kathy Jackson, 32, said she works up

to thirty hours a week to support herself and her father. Ms Jackson earns minimum wage with no benefits. "I really haven't made up my mind [on what to do]. The reality of it hasn't hit."

✪ Dawn Hintzel, a legal secretary and a customer of Wal-Mart says, "It makes me very angry to think they could walk into Hearne ten years ago, set up shop, drive all the other retail business out, and then turn around and leave us holding the bag."

As previously mentioned, Wal-Mart closed its store in Hearne in 1990, and I thought you'd like to know what has happened to the town since then.

I talked to druggist Archer Hoyt, who inherited his drugstore from his father and grandfather. Archer had a beautiful success story, with an expanding store—until Wal-Mart opened a prescription pharmacy at its Hearne location.

Archer fought back with lower prices on everything, but the profits shrunk, almost to nothing. Archer then started advertising strongly on his delivery service, which Wal-Mart couldn't furnish, and started offering thirty-day credit terms to his older customers. Finally, Archer gained back about a third of the business he lost, but it has been flat from that point on. He'll stay in business, but there will be no fourth generation to follow.

The rest of the Hearne merchants have probably fared worse than Archer. Much of the downtown is boarded up—and likely to stay that way. The young people who might have taken over if there had never been a Wal-Mart have moved on to the cities, and who wants to open a store in Hearne anyway, when most of the town is now driving to the new supercenter in nearby College Station?

Hearne, a town of about 6,000, has two large manufacturing plants almost in the city limits, but, seemingly, most other wage earners are now accustomed to shopping in the nearby city with its much, much brighter lights and that comparatively new Wal-Mart supercenter.

"Now, believe it or not," Archer laments, "you can't even buy a white shirt—or even underwear—in this town that once had several thriving dry goods stores."

Bottom line on the Hearne story: Over a ten-year period, the town lost so many of its merchants that Wal-Mart was the only source in town for scores of items a person needs to operate a household. Hearne was a town on crutches, with only one place to buy its needs— at whatever price that store wanted to sell. Then, even that little city's crutches were booted out from under it!

The way to kick up the amount of sales per square foot is to offer more goods and services in a single location, so that location (the Wal-Mart supercenter) comes away with a larger share of the consumer's dollar. Supercenters are more efficient than the standard-issue Wal-Mart store; that is, when a customer leaves a Wal-Mart supercenter, that customer takes home fewer consumer dollars than when leaving a typical Wal-Mart, because he or she has also done the grocery shopping, the banking, prescription drug and eyeglass purchases, car maintenance, and any number of other errands right there in the supercenter.

This is all just cherry pie for Wal-Mart, but think about the way the landscape is starting to look for poor us: Every fifty miles or so a great big shiny does-it-all Wal-Mart, and nothing, nothing, NOTHING in between. Where is competitive pricing going to be then, I wonder, when there are no competitors around? This nightmare vision is extreme, granted, but it's Wal-Mart's most cherished dream. Bank on it.

Wal-Mart Ordered to Pay Ex-Worker $50 Million in Sexual Harassment Case

So squawked a headline from my local paper that deserves to be passed on. Happened in Warsaw, Missouri. Pamela Kimsey and two other women who still work at the store testified that their supervisor and other male employees pinched and kicked them. Wal-Mart will appeal of course, and the abused ladies will be lucky to get more than "time off" money in the final settlement, I'd bet.

International Expansion

One of the strategies that Wal-Mart apparently looks at to keep up its philosophy of growth at any price seems like nothing short of global domination. In a feature article in the 1997 stockholders' report entitled "A 'Global' Brand," Wal-Mart celebrates the growth of its international division. With over 300 locations and more than 50,000 employees outside the United States, the international division saw its first profitable year in fiscal 1997. Sales were in excess of $5 billion, and there's now a Wal-

Mart presence in eight countries (that's Argentina, Brazil, Canada, China, Mexico, Puerto Rico, and Indonesia—and the United States, of course). Wal-Mart CEO David Glass estimates international sales may be 10 percent of the company's total sales in five years.

And I can tell our Canadian and Mexican neighbors that they, especially, will be up against the Wal when this happens. On second thought, I think they already know it. Wal-Mart started its push into Canada in 1994 when it bought out the Woolco chain of stores there—122 stores in all. Woolco was transformed into Wal-Mart in less than a year, and Wal-Mart now dominates Canada's discount retail market. Wal-Mart's trading partner in Mexico is that country's largest retailer.

According to the 1997 shareholders' report, "it is Wal-Mart's emphasis on serving its home town—wherever that may be—that makes Wal-Mart travel so well." Makes you cringe, doesn't it? When you know the "home town" it really serves is Wal-Mart Headquarters, Bentonville, Arkansas, USA. Here's another good one: "Community involvement, responding to local needs, merchandise preferences, and buying locally are all hall-marks of the international Wal-Marts, just as they are in the United States." Really, now—didn't I tell you this report is a hoot and a half to read? I'd like to take a minute to look at just what that might mean to folks without a knowledge of how Wal-Mart really operates.

COMMUNITY INVOLVEMENT

The pledge of community involvement puts me in mind of a certain letter to the editor of *American Forests*, telling about a Wal-Mart store in Lawrence, Kansas, that got a great deal of favorable publicity for having a recycling center at the back of the store. "I used the recycling center regularly, as did many others," writes the editor's correspondent. "I use the past tense because the store has stopped accepting plastic and other hard-to-recycle materials. I see this as a classic bait-and-switch move—having snagged customers and gotten favorable publicity," the retailer dropped the actual operation of the project like a bored child drops a toy.

Capitalist Pigs

Human-rights activist Harry Wu, recently released from a Chinese prison for protesting policies of the country's Communist regime, led a rally at a Wal-Mart store in Auburn, Washington, to protest the retailer's sale of products made in China. Mr. Wu alleges that Wal-Mart has bought products *directly from Chinese military companies.*

T'ain't Fair

I've often wondered, but will never know, just how many tax experts they have there at Wal-Mart headquarters. Enough, for sure, to find every tax dodge.

I note in the July 23, 1997, issue of the *Wall Street Journal* that the Bentonville, Arkansas discounter is closing down forty-eight of its sixty-one Bud's Discount Stores and taking a pretax charge of $40 million to $50 million in its fiscal quarter ending July 31.

The fact that the subsidiary stores were only marginally profitable doesn't enter the picture. But a loophole does exist for closures that will temporarily displace the 1,200 Bud's employees working in these forty-eight stores. Ah, to be able to afford a staff of CPAs to make the world's richest family even richer!

RESPONDING TO LOCAL NEEDS

I've scratched my head trying to come up with an instance when Wal-Mart has been known to respond thoughtfully and generously to any specific local need that is not its own. Couldn't find one, but here's a great example of Wal-Mart's actually anticipating a local need that no one even imagined existed. Bike dealer Phil Slattery sits on the Design Review Board in his home town, and he was interested to hear why a Wal-Mart exec appearing before the board wanted permission to build two 300-square-foot signs on the streets leading to the store. "Why so big?" asked Phil. Well, said the guy, "Our study indicates that the signs will enhance the natural beauty of the area." Imagine that! Phil asked to see the explanation of this "enhancement" in writing; to date he hasn't seen a thing. (Phil, when you get it, send me a copy. I'll bet it's worth at least one chuckle.)

Same Theme, Different Country

From *USA Today:* "Wal-Mart's 4.7-acre supercenter in Mexico City was (recently) closed for a day because of import violations. Two Mexican newspapers reported that 13,707 products in Wal-Mart's inventory didn't comply with import-labeling rules." Shame, shame, you naughty discounters.

MERCHANDISE PREFERENCES

What "merchandise preferences" means, I think, is that Wal-Mart's managers look at what is already selling in the town, bring it into stock, sell it cheaper (sometimes for less than cost) until nearly all competitors are squashed flatter than a mosquito at a Fourth of July picnic, then to sell it at any price they damn please.

BUYING LOCALLY

Buying locally does not necessarily mean paying locally. In July 1994, *Inc.* magazine had a feature on Wal-Mart that revealed that the retailer was known to string along local suppliers for up to ten weeks. Can you imagine staying in business if you did that to your townspeople?

Canadians! Mexicans! Argentineans! Brazilians! Write to me and let me know how your fair countries are holding up under Wal-Mart's invasion. If you can't send me some damn tart anecdotes in short order, I'll eat my hat.

Indeed, I just read a front-page story in the *Wall Street Journal* reporting on how hard Wal-Mart is fighting to get accepted in South American and Asian countries, and I quote the *Journal* here: "The company's insistence on doing things the Wal-Mart way has apparently alienated local suppliers and employees." I, for one, can't wait to hear how the foreign fur is a-flying!

Other articles in Wal-Mart's annual report indicate that the company is putting a lot of eggs in the baskets (so to speak) of its new computerized inventory control systems. These are just being rolled out and look to be Wal-Mart's new great hope of keeping costs under control. I haven't heard anything from customers and suppliers about this new system yet, but I expect to. I quote Randy Mott, senior vice president and chief information officer of Wal-Mart: "We may be talking about state-of-the-art computer systems, but the way we manage them is pure Wal-Mart." If that's the case, Randy, it means that these gadgets will figure in their fair share of tales of outrage and degradation, Wal-Mart-style. I'll keep you posted.

12 WAYS YOU CAN FIGHT BACK

Wal-Mart is big, mean, and ugly, but not always invincible. Dozens of cities have turned the big bully away; hundreds of small businesses have fought hard and smart against Sam's empire. Whether you are a retailer competing with Sam and Company, a supplier selling to them, a citizen concerned about Wal-Mart coming to town, or a consumer concerned about your own bottom line and the well-being of your town, here are just a few ways you might get the satisfaction of a battle well-waged in your dealings with Wal-Mart.

Retailers

Predatory pricing getting you down? Try one or more of the following solutions. Give Wal-Mart hell!

1. MINIMIZE YOUR COMPETITIVE EDGE

That's right. Limit your exposure to Wal-Mart's competition by taking yourself out of competition as much as you can. One of the smartest merchants I know emphasizes that you can't—no way—compete with Wal-Mart by carrying the same brand-name merchandise. Simply visit your nearest Wal-Mart on a regular basis and make a mental note of the brands the discounter is stocking. Then stock a competing brand.

2. THROW YOUR WEIGHT AROUND

Eleven Argentinean vendors are refusing to sell to Wal-Mart, citing pressure from long-established retailers who carry the same lines Wal-Mart is discounting. (Wal-Mart's response, according to the *Wall Street Journal,* was typically charming: "[We] may have to import merchandise into Argentina and take business away from local workers.") This approach may not be viable for a number of small guys, but you may just want to consider your vendor relationships in this light: they may be just as sick of dealing with Wal-Mart as can be.

3. TRY SOME TRUTH IN ADVERTISING

Do you have something that Wal-Mart doesn't? (You bet you do.) Advertise it! Clay Hardy of Ronco Bicycles in Havelock, North Carolina, took the following tack when Wal-Mart came to his town. He put out a sign reading,

"What does the Wal-Mart bike mechanic look like?" Since then, he reports, he has repaired, adjusted, or assembled more then 500 bikes that were bought from the mega-retailer.

4. JUST SAY NO

The next time you go to an exposition, ask exhibitors whether they are selling to discounters. If the answer is yes, chances are you won't get a good discount. Bonus point: if you decide not to place an order, you may want to tell the exhibitor that this was a factor in your decision.

5. USE GUERRILLA TACTICS

Check out how one of South America's biggest discounters, Carrefour, is giving Sam Hell, with a capital *H*. According to the *Wall Street Journal*, "When Wal-Mart's new store prints a flier advertising bargains, the nearby Carrefour responds in just a few hours offering the same products for a few cents less—and the flyers are handed out at the entrance to the Wal-Mart parking lot." Hip! Hip! Hooray!

If you have the determination, the imagination, and the guts for a guerrilla campaign like this (even if it's a one-time deal, done on a smaller scale), you could poke a nice-sized stick in Wal-Mart's eye and have yourself some fun in the bargain.

A Word to the Wise: Check Your Receipts

A family friend walked into an Arkansas Wal-Mart store one day, carrying the company's monthly "specials" circular. On checking out he noted the store's computerized listing of purchases had three overcharges. He demanded to see the manager. After he'd been waiting some time, the manager appeared, and when he did our friend asked:

"What would you do if one of your employees caught me with three shoplifted items?"

"I'd call store security, and they in turn would probably call the police," the manager responded.

"Well, check my purchase tape and your circular's quoted prices; then perhaps I should call the police myself and tell them you're 'shoplifting' from me."

The manager was temporarily at a loss for words. "All you're talking about is a computer error. I'll ask the girl here to refund your money."

My buddy, remembering a TV program that researched such errors and found that only one in four customers double-checked and asked for refunds, concluded that he saw little difference in whose pocket was picked— the store's or the customer's.

Multiply just that one person's overcharges several times a day at 2,500-plus Walton operations and you've just got to project that the company makes many, many extra millions a year because so few of their customers check their purchase tapes.

The moral of the story? You guessed it.

6. FIGHT MARKETING AGREEMENTS
THAT FREEZE YOU OUT

According to our local paper, the *Star-Telegram,* Fort Worth–area record store owner Bill Sowers launched a protest against the rock group Aerosmith in 1997. The group's label had made an exclusive deal with Wal-Mart to distribute its new EP. Feeling burned and righteous, Bill S. returned his entire stock of the group's other albums to the label. The cost to him will probably be about $1,000 to $2,000 in sales, all told, but God bless him!

For other store owners caught in a similar problem, here's a less gonzo approach: Enlist the help of your loyal customers. Publicize what's going on. Put out some fliers or a sign letting folks know of the cozy agreement between Wal-Mart and the record label—and telling them whom to write to if this ticks them off (give the label's address and e-mail).

If customers in your store were actually looking for the new Aerosmith EP (or whatever), then they'll know why they can't find it, and they might be pretty upset— but not with you. (Some of them might just go over to Wal-Mart and buy the damn thing there, but you weren't going to get that sale anyway, were you?) Your sign makes it clear who's to blame, and the label might actually get some feedback from people they listen to: consumers. There's always a hope that, shown a downside, they'll be less ready to pull this crap the next time.

Suppliers

If you sell to Wal-Mart and they are killing you on the margin, there's just one thing I can recommend that you consider:

7. DON'T PLAY

According to the *Wall Street Journal,* the toy manufacturer Step2 has decided not to supply to Wal-Mart, joining a number of manufacturers who do not deal with Wal-Mart and other mega-retailers with "mighty retail clout." Apparently the manufacturers simply can't stomach the huge discounts at which the retailers sell their products (not to mention the other squirrelly things Wal-Mart does to its vendors—see chapter 3).

Citizens and Planning Boards

If a Wal-Mart or another big discounter is sniffing around your town, look out! Now's the time when you still have power, and it's time to prepare.

8. OVERHAUL YOUR TOWN'S COMPREHENSIVE PLAN

Check out the steps outlined by the Lancaster County Planning Commission on page 21 of this book. These four steps, taken with foresight and thoughtfulness, will go far toward "Wal-Mart-proofing" your town. Warning: these steps take time and are best for those towns that don't have a fight right on the horizon.

9. MAKE ZONING APPROVAL PROCESSES MORE STRICT

This is a corollary to *8*, above. Wal-Marts are invariably built away from downtown, often in an as-yet-undeveloped area. This means that, in order for a Wal-Mart to be built, the developer who owns the building will have to get zoning changes so they can get sewer, drainage, and traffic needs met.

Now, some forward-looking local merchants with political clout are asking city councils to rewrite the city's bylaws to demand that any request for zoning changes must be approved by at least a two-thirds vote of the city council. This would certainly tend to make a quiet and sneaky incursion by Wal-Mart much more difficult.

10. HOW ABOUT A GOOD OLD-FASHIONED PETITION DRIVE?

This tried-and-true (and easy to do) form of protest was recently part of Westford, Massachusetts's, drive to keep out Wal-Mart. Many of the 500 folks who signed the petition went a step further, wearing "If they build it, we won't come" buttons in the weeks before the petition passed. Find out at your city hall what the petition protocol is in your town, and get together some clipboards and some pens.

11. RUN FOR OFFICE

Jerry Greenfield, of Ben & Jerry's Ice Cream fame, did just this in his town of Williston, Vermont: he ran for city office for the express purpose of voting against a mall that would have Wal-Mart as one of its tenants. If you care enough about your town to take a major stake in the future of its development, a local office might just be the place for you to do some good work. It is surprisingly easy to run for office on the local level, and it's something to think about if you are ready to take the next step in civic commitment.

Consumers

12. COMPARISON SHOP

I'd tell you to check prices and compare, but Virginia Berger of Spring Hill, Florida, tried to do just that and was told by the Wal-Mart staff that jotting down their prices was "against store policy." Whew! Now why could that be? Could it be because study after study has shown that Wal-Mart's prices, for the most part, are not lower than discount competitors, that they are, in many cases, substantially higher?

Well, you may have to use your excellent memory (or a mini tape recorder), but if you have any doubt about it, find out for yourself. Most of us know, when we are making a big-ticket purchase, to shop around. But what about those mid- and lower-priced items? So many of us depend on ads to do the comparing for us, but there's an obvious problem with that.

If you want to determine which store or stores in your area actually has the lowest prices overall, why not check it out? Many of us have the minor luxury of not having to bargain-hunt on everything we buy, from toilet paper to mac-and-cheese, but it would be nice to know who we can trust, in general, to be giving us a good price. And it may not be the much-hyped discounter.

Of course, it is this kind of conscious buying that Wal-Mart allows you to escape entirely. Everything all in one place! One-stop shopping! If not the lowest price, at least one that looks fairly competitive! Just remember what kinds of things you are giving away when you give away your power as a consumer to the big discounters- and what they are reaping in return when too many of us start thinking this way: massive profits and huge growth; the blind arrogance of a mighty corporation; and the ruin of the texture of so much of small-town America's commerce and society.

Old Sam's Cloud of Fear

Here's a January, 1998 story from the Dallas News date-lined Bentonville, Arkansas that says the townsfolk are just now-five years after Sam's death- daring to build homes that would have been expected at their income levels as long as ten years ago. Sam's example of extremely frugal living flowed downhill, either by insistence or fear. "Wal-Mart executives and vendors avoided sprawling homes, designer clothes, fancy cars, and watches more expensive than engagement rings. Those who didn't were usually chastised."

Poor old Sam. The guy who refused to pay more than $5 for a haircut, or $100 for a suit. At long, long last Wal-Mart execs and vendors who live in Bentonville are enjoying things they can well afford. And come to think of it, isn't living life to the fullest why thee and me worked so hard for so many years?

A&E Biography on Sam Walton Reveals His True Nature

This writer, a real fan of those biographies shown regularly on the Arts & Entertainment network, was particularly interested in the December, 1997 program that spotlighted the Arkansas discounter. It gave me a chill to see how cold-blooded he really was, even with all I knew to date.

For starters, the biography said he was "the man who made small-town merchants virtually obsolete."

A&E portrayed him as a man who liked to pilot his own plane when he visited his stores. When he came into town, he liked to fly low before landing, and was frequently warned by the airport's control not to "buzz" the area. The man who wrote his biography, who rode with him several times, asked Sam what he did when he got those warnings. "I just cut off the radio," Sam said.

The segment also said that when Sam made his first big money he bought majority interest in a Bentonville state bank. And, as we understood the commentary, loaned himself money at the very lowest possible interest rate.

Sam's plan for stock options was also mentioned. Only the managers were to share in the original plan. Sam believed that only the "top guns" were in a position to help him get richer and richer. His wife, Helen, maintained that all the "workers in the trenches" should also benefit. Helen finally-the key word here is finally-shamed Sam into enlarging his stock plan.

And, finally, the A&E hour told how anti-union Sam was. Bitter. Bitter. Bitter. When one of his giant distribution centers threatened a vote to unionize, old Sam loudly said he had 500 applicants ready to take their jobs. The threat worked.

The long and the short of it for me is, I hate Wal-Mart. I'll never set foot in another of those emporiums of crap as long as I live, and I'll fight them until the day I die.

But you may choose to shop at Wal-Mart; you may even be happy to have a Wal-Mart in your town. There are legitimate reasons to shop there, and real reasons why people welcome Wal-Mart on the land.

All I ask is that if you decide in favor of Wal-Mart— whether you're shopping for a barbecue grill there or permitting the mega-retailer to build in your town—just know what you are choosing, and know what you are choosing to give up and what you may allow to be destroyed, if only by being silent.

Readers

Yes, I'm working on a sequel to this book. I'd like to hear about your most unpleasant experience in dealing with Wal-Mart, and I'll pay $100 for every letter that's published. So write to me or, if you'd like, just use the front and back of this page, tear it out, and mail it to Bill Quinn, P.O. Box 1570, Fort Worth, TX 76101

Former Wal-Mart Employees

You're invited to use this tear-out page to tell us why you told Wal-Mart to take the job you had and shove it. I'll pay $100 for every letter that's published in a sequel to this book. Send your letter to Bill Quinn, P.O. Box 1570, Fort Worth, TX 76101

Independent Merchants

All merchants who have been put out of business, or storekeepers who are suffering from Wal-Mart's business tactics, are urged to tell their stories. I'll pay $100 for any letter published in a sequel to this book. I'd prefer if you write to me on letterhead, but you can also just write on the page below. Either way, send it to Bill Quinn, P.O. Box 1570, Fort Worth, TX 76101

Vendors/Suppliers

Financially, I know you've suffered the most as a result of Walton Enterprises. All I ask from you now is that you write to me about your mistreatment. I guarantee that your letter will be kept 101% confidential, unless you tell me personally that it's okay to publish. My address is Bill Quinn, P.O. Box 1570, Fort Worth, TX 76101